Fathers of the Faith
Saint Athanasius

FATHERS
of the FAITH

SAINT ATHANASIUS

Mike Aquilina

Our Sunday Visitor
Huntington, Indiana

Nihil Obstat
Msgr. Michael Heintz, Ph.D.
Censor Librorum

Imprimatur
Kevin C. Rhoades
Bishop of Fort Wayne–South Bend
March 6, 2023

The *Nihil Obstat* and *Imprimatur* are official declarations that a book is free from doctrinal or moral error. It is not implied that those who have granted the *Nihil Obstat* and *Imprimatur* agree with the contents, opinions, or statements expressed.

Except where noted, the Scripture citations used in this work are taken from the *Revised Standard Version of the Bible — Second Catholic Edition* (Ignatius Edition), copyright © 1965, 1966, 2006 National Council of the Churches of Christ in the United States of America. Used by permission. All rights reserved.

Every reasonable effort has been made to determine copyright holders of excerpted materials and to secure permissions as needed. If any copyrighted materials have been inadvertently used in this work without proper credit being given in one form or another, please notify Our Sunday Visitor in writing so that future printings of this work may be corrected accordingly.

Our Sunday Visitor Publishing Division, Our Sunday Visitor, Inc., 200 Noll Plaza, Huntington, IN 46750; www.osv.com; 1-800-348-2440

ISBN: 978-1-68192-397-0 (Inventory No. T2774)
1. RELIGION—Christianity—Saints & Sainthood.
2. RELIGION—Christian Church—History.
3. RELIGION—Christianity—Catholic.
eISBN: 978-1-68192-398-7
LCCN: 2023936568

Cover and interior design: Amanda Falk
Cover image: Crosiers and AdobeStock

PRINTED IN THE UNITED STATES OF AMERICA

For Father Tom Weinandy

Contents

A Note about Dates

You'll see years mentioned here and there in this book, and you should know that they might be wrong. In the eventful life of Saint Athanasius, different historians have come to different conclusions about when this or that happened. But they usually differ by only two or three years at the most. Take the years as showing the rough chronology of events. Don't take them as absolutely accurate dates.

Foreword

In the entire history of the Church, it would be hard to find a more indispensable bishop than St. Athanasius of Alexandria.

Arius, the arch-heretic, professed that the Son of God was a creature and so was not truly God as the Father is God. This denial not only negated the Trinity but also nullified the Incarnation. In AD 325, the Council of Nicaea declared that the Son of God was begotten and not made and that, therefore, he was of the same substance (*homoousios*) with the Father. It was this divine Son who came to exist as man and suffered and died under Pontius Pilate for our sins and for our salvation. After such a decisive affirmation, one would think that this issue was definitively closed once and for all. The sixty years following the council, however, were years of political, ecclesial, and theological chaos. In the midst of such bedlam, one man staunchly and faithfully stayed true to the Nicene Creed. That man was Athanasius. When many, if not most, of the bishops waffled and waivered, when the followers of Arius appeared to be winning the day, and in the midst of being exiled five times, Athanasius was a lone voice crying out in the wilderness of heresy: Jesus Christ is the eternal Son of the Father; he is indeed consubstantial, one in being, with the Father; and it is this divine Son who became incarnate for our salvation. It was Athanasius against the world!

Mike Aquilina, in this biography, does justice to Saint Athanasius's heroic and tumultuous life. Mike writes with great clarity and is meticulous in his research, and for this he is renowned. He provides not only the facts surrounding Athanasius's life but also an authentic interpretation of the historical events surrounding his life and what Athanasius does and accomplishes. Moreover, while treating serious doctrinal concerns, such as the divinity of Jesus, Mike is never boring to read. His writing is filled with vitality, and so the reader becomes immersed in Athanasius's life — with all of its ups and downs, its defeats and victories. One cannot help but root for Athanasius while yet fearful of what danger he will next encounter. Simply put, Mike's biography of Saint Athanasius is both serious in nature and momentous in content and also entertaining and a joy to read. The reader will come to love Saint Athanasius and may even become his friend.

Although Mike has written in these pages a life of Athanasius, it is, as intimated above, filled with doctrinal importance, for the doctrines of the Trinity and the Incarnation are what make Athanasius who his is. He is forever identified with these central Christian mysteries of the Faith. These mysteries were alive for Athanasius. He was imbued with them. They were not, as some would contend today, "dead dogmas." Athanasius, with all of his heart and mind, perceived that the Father, the Son, and the Holy Spirit not only possess the eternal fullness of life and love among themselves but have also showered an abundance of life and love on all they have created and redeemed. For Athanasius, if Jesus were not truly the Father's divine Son, then our salvation could not be attained, for only God can redeem humankind. Moreover, if the divine Son did not truly exist as an authentic man, then he could not free us from the sin that resides in our humanity, nor could he vanquish our death, the curse of sin. Likewise, the Son of God must rise gloriously from the dead as man, for only then could we come to share in his risen and divine life — the life of the indwelling and transforming Holy Spirit. Thus, Mike, in narrating the life of Athanasius, is instructing the reader of the salvific importance of these divine mysteries — the mysteries that Athanasius treasured.

I know of no other biography of Saint Athanasius that is theologically sound and historically accurate as well as being accessible to a popular audience. For this achievement, Mike Aquilina deserves our thanks and praise.

Thomas G. Weinandy, OFM, Capuchin

1.
The Boy Who Played Bishop

There's a story about Saint Athanasius that probably isn't true. But like a lot of stories that probably aren't true, it tells us more truth than mere facts could give us.

The story goes like this: Alexander, bishop of Alexandria, is standing on the beach. He has just finished a Mass on the anniversary of the martyrdom of his predecessor Peter. Now he's waiting for some friends, and they haven't shown up yet, so his attention is wandering a bit, and he notices a group of boys playing on the beach.

Something about what they're doing attracts his attention. It doesn't take long for him to realize they're playing church. One of the boys has taken the role of the bishop, and they're acting out the ceremonies very accurately.

Alexander smiles.

Then he starts to listen.

Suddenly, he's not smiling anymore.

"I baptize you in the name of the Father, and of the Son, and of the Holy Spirit," he hears the bishop boy saying.

Quickly he signals some of his priests, and they walk over to the boys. Of course, the boys stop what they're doing. They don't know what's going on, but it looks as if they're in trouble.

"What were you doing?" Alexander asks.

Silence.

"I asked you what you were doing," he repeats.

"Nothin'," one of the boys says quietly.

"Look, I don't want to have to spank anybody. I don't want to have to *tell your mothers*. I just need to know what you were doing."

Finally, one of the boys speaks up. "We were just playing," he says. "Athanasius was the bishop, and he was doing baptisms." He points at one of the other boys to indicate that, really, it's all his fault, whatever it is.

So the one who was performing the baptism must be the boy called Athanasius. Alexander turns to him with a look that's hard for the boy to interpret.

"Did I do something wrong?" little Athanasius asks quietly.

Alexander considers his response for a moment. "The problem," he says at last, "is that you did everything *right*."

Those were real baptisms, Alexander explains. Athanasius got the words and the actions exactly right. His young friends are full members of the Christian Church now, so Alexander will have to make sure they're properly catechized. And no more playing baptism because it could cause all kinds of trouble.

Is the Story True?

That's the story as it was told decades later, about thirty years after Athanasius died.

Is this story true? It's hard to know. We have some serious reasons for doubting it, though: the numbers don't seem to work out. Peter died in 311, one in the last wave of martyrs in the last great persecution. Alexander became bishop in 312, so celebration of the

anniversary of Peter's martyrdom could have been no
earlier than that. Sozomen, the church historian, sets the
scene this way: "It was the custom of the Alexandrians
to celebrate with great pomp an annual festival in honor
of one of their bishops named Peter, who had suffered
martyrdom. Alexander, who then conducted the church,
engaged in the celebration of this festival."[1] That makes
it sound as though the "custom" had been going on for
a while.

Almost everyone agrees that Athanasius was born
between 295 and 299. Even if he was born as late as 298,
and even if the celebration was the first anniversary of
Peter's death, that would make him fourteen years old at
the earliest possible time for that story — a bit old to be
playing games like a little boy.

Where did the story come from? The first known
mention of it is in the Latin historian Rufinus, which is
where Sozomen got it. Rufinus doesn't tell us where he
got it. Rufinus translated Eusebius's *Ecclesiastical History* into Latin and added two books of his own to bring
Eusebius up to date, but he was not the careful historian
Eusebius was. Eusebius looked up original documents
and cited his sources; Rufinus just told any old story
he happened to hear. Of course, it's possible that Rufinus told a true story and got some of the circumstances

wrong. Maybe Alexander was only a priest at the time, and maybe the occasion wasn't the anniversary of Peter's martyrdom. But as it stands, the story doesn't seem to hold water.

So why begin with a story that probably isn't even true?

The fact that people told this story about Athanasius tells us what kind of person they thought he was. In particular, it shows us two things everybody knew about Athanasius: First, he was brilliant even when he was young. Second, he always made sure to get everything exactly right. He never deviated from Christian truth — not by a single iota.

Athanasius against the World

Athanasius is one of those truly pivotal figures in the chronicles of the world. The world remembers him as Athanasius the Great and Athanasius the Father of Orthodoxy. He was one of those figures who stood athwart history, yelling *stop*, at a time when no one else was inclined to do so. He stood alone, and so he appeared to be foolhardy and his mission quixotic.

One of his opponents described the situation in mocking terms. It was "Athanasius against the world."

Athanasius didn't care. He stood his ground and

made history do his bidding — or, rather, heaven's bidding.

So his life from young adult on is very well documented. But no one really knows anything about his childhood. The only light we get on his early years is that story from Rufinus, and — as we've seen — that story probably isn't literally true, no matter how much of the truth about Athanasius it conveys in a metaphorical way. Aside from that, we have only the barest hints.

Family and Education

There's a tradition that says Athanasius came from a wealthy family, and that makes some sense. He had a very good education — the kind you usually got only if your parents were rich enough to pay for it.

His parents were Christians. We don't get a conversion story for Athanasius; it would certainly have become part of the legend if there had been a conversion story. Instead, St. Gregory Nazianzen, in a eulogy of Athanasius, gives us a glancing reference to his education: "He was brought up, from the first, in religious habits and practices, after a brief study of literature and philosophy, so that he might not be utterly unskilled in such subjects, or ignorant of matters which he had determined to despise."[2] So he had a standard education in the classics, but at home he learned how to be a good Christian. It's obvious from his writings that he received a profound education in Scripture as well as the arts associated with argument. He had an unusual command of both the Old Testament and the New.

At some point, he also learned some practical lessons in Christian asceticism from the holy men in the desert — especially Saint Anthony, the father of all monks, who would become a lifelong friend and fearless supporter of Athanasius. Years later, Athanasius wrote Anthony's biography — one of the most-read books in Christian history and one that would have a profound influence on monasticism in both the East and the West. His description of the settlement of desert ascetics sounds nostalgic and wistful, as if it was the life he really wished for himself — the life that someone who was thrust into the public life of the Church could never have:

> The monasteries now were like so many sacred tabernacles, full of divine choirs, singing and delighting in holy conversation, and fasting and praying, and exulting in the hope of future goods, and working to give alms, and exercising mutual love and unanimous agreement among themselves. So that you might really see there

a land of piety and righteousness by itself: for there was neither an injurious nor an injured person nor any complaint of the oppressor, but a multitude of ascetics, having one and the same ardor for virtue — so much so that someone who saw such monasteries could not keep from crying out, as we read: "How fair are your tents, O Jacob, your encampments, O Israel! Like valleys that stretch afar, like gardens beside a river, like aloes that the Lord has planted, like cedar trees beside the waters." (Numbers 24:5–6)[3]

Physical Description

As for what Athanasius was like physically, we know that in later life, he was a small man, but he was energetic even when he was older. That would come in handy when he was running for his life. One of his worst enemies would later describe Athanasius as a "contemptible puppet,"[4] suggesting that his small size was a well-known identifying characteristic.

And that's as much as we know about Athanasius until the year 312 (the earliest possible year for that story about the boys playing bishop), when, still a teenager, he was ordained a reader — the lowest level of clerical orders in the East. The man who ordained him was Alexander, the bishop in the story.

It's likely that Athanasius had been getting guidance from Alexander as he grew. While still a teen, he became a confidant and adviser to the bishop, which strongly suggests that Alexander had known him for a long time and recognized his unusual talents.

And those first days after the end of the Roman persecution were days when a bishop could use a lot of help.

The Background: Persecution to Liberation

A little bit of background: For two and a half centuries, Christianity had been an illegal cult in the Roman Empire. Even in the Acts of the Apostles, we already see local persecutions of Christians, but it was Nero who established it as a legal principle that Christianity was a crime. Looking for someone to blame for the great fire in Rome in the year 64, he settled on the Christians, because they were a weird cult that people didn't trust anyway.

From that time on, Christianity was illegal, and technically the penalty was death. But the penalty wasn't always enforced. In fact, it wasn't usually enforced — especially after the emperor Trajan made a don't-ask, don't-tell rule that instructed officials not to go looking for Christians. There were occasional bursts of fierce persecution, when martyrs made converts by their example of heroic fortitude, and the Church grew. But there were long periods of peace, when ordinary Christians made converts by their example of a better way of life, and the Church grew. No matter what happened, the Church grew. By about the year 300, it was probably the largest single religious group in the empire — and still illegal.

The last and worst persecution began in 303 under Diocletian, who was trying to put the Roman Empire back together after decades of civil war. It would continue until 312 under his successors Galerius and Maximinus Daia.

This persecution was organized with bureaucratic efficiency, and it was ruthless. House-to-house searches looked for Christian books to burn. Everyone, with the exception of Jews (whose ancient religion was weird to the Romans but was legal because it was ancient), had to make a pagan sacrifice to the emperor's genius. It didn't have to be much of a sacrifice — just a pinch of incense, provided for you at the site, and you were done. The important thing was that you had to have the certificate that showed you were in compliance. And real Christians couldn't get one, because real Christians couldn't betray Christ with even the tiniest pinch of incense to a false god.

But when they were threatened with torture, thousands of nominal Christians did give up and get their certificates. There was also, as you might expect, an underground business in forged certificates, which some Christians thought of as a way of keeping alive in good conscience but which others believed were just as much a betrayal of Christ. Of course, thousands of others didn't give in, and many of them died in agony for their resistance. The perfectly reasonable Roman governors always made it clear that the tortures would stop if the victim would just curse Christ and make the legally mandated token sacrifice, and if the Christians were going to be so stubborn after that, they deserved whatever they got.

Meanwhile, the empire was descending into civil war again. Six emperors were rampaging across the landscape with huge armies. After a few years of stability under Diocletian, the Roman world had fallen back into its usual chaos.

And then came Constantine.

Constantine and the Cross in the Sky

The story told by Constantine himself was that just before he made his final assault on the tyrant Maxentius, who held Rome at the time, he saw in the sky a vision of a cross with the words "In this sign you will conquer." The next day, his army fought under the banner of the cross — and won.

That was in 312. In 313, Constantine and the Eastern emperor Licinius issued the Edict of Milan, making every religion legal. And Constantine, the more powerful emperor (and soon the only one, since he and Licinius had a falling out and Licinius lost), was a Christian.

Suddenly, the Christian Church went from illegal cult to favored religion of the empire.

This was the heady atmosphere in which Athanasius began his clerical career as a reader. And you would think that, at last, all the troubles were over, and the Church could just go about her business unmolested.

But it wasn't as simple as that.

2.
Alexander's Right-Hand Man

By the time he was in his early twenties, young Athanasius was already making a name in the world as a theologian. His first known works are a pair of books that are today considered classics of Christian theology: *Against the Heathens* and *Oration on the Incarnation*. In them, Athanasius is already an intellectual force to reckon with. The second especially is considered a classic and fundamental text in the field of Christology.

From our historical point of view, what's most striking about them is that they show no awareness of the storm that was about to break over Alexandria.

Alexandria

To understand the rest of the story, we need to know a little about Alexandria in Egypt. It was founded by Alexander the Great — one of many cities he founded and named after himself, and which was, by far, the most successful. After the empire of Alexander broke into three pieces, Alexandria was the capital of Egypt, ruled by the Ptolemies, Macedonians who soon made it the commercial and intellectual jewel of the Mediterranean.

Alexandria had the only good Mediterranean harbor in Egypt, so all the trade between Egypt and the rest of the Mediterranean world went through the city, making it incalculably rich. The Ptolemies were also keen on making it a center of learning. The famous library, often destroyed and often restocked, tried to keep a copy of every book in the world. Around it grew something very like a modern university, where the best of every kind of learning could be had. Alexandria was a magic name, like Harvard or Oxford today: The pagan historian Ammianus Marcellinus said that "it is sufficient as a recommendation for any medical man to say that he was educated in Alexandria."[1]

Alexandria also became the second most important center of Jewish culture, next to Jerusalem — and became the most important after Jerusalem was destroyed in the year 70. It was in Alexandria that the Septuagint, the Greek translation of the Hebrew Bible that was familiar to the New Testament writers, was made.

Christianity came early to Alexandria. Tradition says that Mark the evangelist founded the church there, and he is counted as the first bishop. Soon Alexandria was the intellectual capital of the Christian world as well as the pagan world and the Jewish world. It was home to the most prestigious school of theology. It produced prodigies such as Clement and Origen, whose brilliant minds accelerated the development of Christian doctrine.

By the time Constantine made Christianity legal, the bishop of Alexandria had become the second most influential Christian bishop in the world. Only the bishop of Rome was more important — and both the bishop of Rome and the bishop of Alexandria were called "pope."

So Alexandria was a magnificent city of stunning intellectual achievements, beautiful buildings, and a diverse population of Christians, pagans, and Jews. It would be delightful to say that they all lived in peace and harmony. But they didn't.

City of Riots

Alexandria was notorious as the city of riots. Other cities frequently had riots too, but Alexandria beat them all. It was "a city which from its own impulses, and without any special cause, is continually agitated by seditious tumults," says our pagan friend Ammianus.[2]

So in addition to all the usual big-city problems, Alexandria was a place where any Christian bishop would have to deal with angry mobs more than once in his career.

At about the time he wrote his first two books, Athanasius was ordained a deacon, and Bishop Alexander took him on as secretary — just in time for the storm to break. The thunderclap came in 318, but the storm had been brewing for a long time before that.

Ready to Fight the Pagans

Those first two books by Athanasius, which really make up one work in two volumes, were addressed to the pagans, who still made up a big part of the population, although their numbers were dwindling generation by generation. His argument in the first volume was that Christianity was the religion of reason, whereas paganism was the religion of folly. Look at the stories about the Greek gods! Could gods possibly act that way? They must have been only men, and not even good men. In fact, they must have been drunk. It's a good sample of what would become his trademark style of argument: He would back his opponents into a corner, cut every possible argument out from under them, and then wither them with sarcasm:

> But perhaps the impious will respond by saying these are just poets' fictions — that poets specialize in making up things that are not true, and telling fictional tales for the pleasure of their hearers. That is why they have composed the stories about gods.
>
> But we can see that this argument is even more superficial than any other from what they themselves think and profess about these matters. For if what is said in the poets is fictitious and false, even the names of Zeus, Cronos, Hera, Ares and the rest must be false. For perhaps, as they say, even the names are fictitious, and, while no such being exists as Zeus, Cronos, or Ares, the poets make them up to deceive their hearers. But if the poets feign the existence of

unreal beings, how is it that they worship them as though they existed?

Or perhaps, once again, they will say that while the names are not fictitious, they ascribe to them fictitious actions. But even this is equally precarious as a defense. For if they made up the actions, doubtless they also made up the names, to which they attributed the actions. Or if they tell the truth about the names, it follows that they tell the truth about the actions, too. …

Or if, as poets, they told falsehoods, and you are maligning them, why did they not also tell falsehoods about the courage of the heroes, and pretend that courageous heroes were cowards, or cowards were courageous heroes? If they made Zeus and Hera into the opposite of what they really are, then they should slanderously accuse Achilles of lacking courage, and celebrate the might of Thersites.* They should say that Odysseus was dull-witted, that Nestor was reckless. They should tell stories of Diomed and Hector acting like women, and Hecuba acting like a man. If this is the way poets write stories, then they should write that way about every

---

*A notorious fool and coward in Homeric lore.

character. But in fact, they kept the truth for
their human characters, while not ashamed to
tell falsehoods about their so-called gods.

And if they argue that they are telling falsehoods about their immoral acts, but that in their
praises, when they speak of Zeus as father of
gods, and as the highest, and the Olympian, and
as reigning in heaven, they are not inventing but
speaking truthfully — this is a plea that not only
I but anybody at all can refute. For the truth will
clearly be against them if we recall our previous
proofs. For while their actions prove them to
be men, the panegyrics upon them go beyond
the nature of men. The two things cancel each
other. It is not the nature of heavenly beings to
act in such ways, and no one can imagine that
beings who do act in such ways are gods.[3]

That Athanasius put all his rhetorical and argumenta-
tive skill into a treatise against the pagans tells us that
the pagans were the people he was concerned about at
the time. Neither he nor Alexander seems to have been
thinking that the biggest threat would come from inside
the Christian Church. But the threat was building.

Not that the bishop saw nothing wrong in his diocese.

The Church in Alexandria had no shortage of problems. But one day in the year 318, the Alexandrian Church awoke to the *big* problem — and by then it was far advanced.

The Martyr's Warning

The signs had been there for some years. The martyred bishop Peter had read them very clearly.

The future Bishop Alexander was a clergyman in Alexandria during the challenging years of the last persecution, and he was a trusted aide to Bishop Peter. In those days, Peter's most vexing problem (it seems) was not the persecution but its aftermath. Many Christians had died as martyrs. Many others, however, had given in to pressure and offered sacrifice to the Roman gods. Later, some regretted their weakness and begged the Church for readmission.

What should the Church do in cases like this? Some churches refused to readmit apostates unless they were in danger of imminent death. Others admitted them only after years of heavy penance. In Alexandria, Peter leaned toward leniency — a policy that was fiercely opposed by a minority of his clergy as well as by Egyptian and Libyan bishops who were under his authority. One of those bishops was a man named Melitius of Lycopolis. Melitius adamantly refused to take back the repentant, and he used Peter's leniency as a reason to question the legitimacy of his authority. This was open rebellion, and Melitius succeeded in persuading twenty-eight other bishops to join his cause. They called themselves the Church of the Martyrs, and they quickly became a parallel church in Egypt and Libya.

Peter, of course, excommunicated the Melitians.

But soon enough, the civil authorities came for Peter, who, in his turn, refused to offer sacrifice. While he was in prison awaiting execution, the Melitians seized the moment to increase their activity. Melitius himself traveled into cities where the bishops were imprisoned, and in each place, he took it upon himself to ordain priests and deacons who might become his supporters.

Two of Peter's most trusted clergymen, Achillas and Alexander, visited him in prison. Peter knew that one of those men would likely be his successor, and he urged them to continue his policies regarding mercy toward the weak and the suppression of the Melitians. He was emphatic on one point in particular: He warned them about a man named Arius, an especially wily supporter of Melitius. Arius was not to be trusted, Peter said, and he should certainly not be readmitted to communion with the Church.

And then Peter went off to die as a martyr.

Now, you'd think that the last words of a martyr would ring with authority in the ears of his hearers. You'd think that Achillas and Alexander would take Peter's warning as their mission and follow it to the letter.

You'd think. But they didn't.

Achillas was chosen as Peter's successor, and quite soon after his installation, he made a hasty reconciliation with Arius. And then he did something inexplicable: He ordained him in rapid succession to the diaconate and then to the priesthood. To top it all off, he assigned this newly ordained priest to serve as pastor at one of the oldest, biggest, and most prestigious churches in the city of Alexandria.

Now, Arius was undeniably a gifted man. Born in Libya, he had gone on to pursue theological studies in the Syrian city of Antioch. He had studied under renowned intellectuals who went on to die as martyrs. He later migrated to Alexandria, where he gained a reputation for asceticism and for his clever teaching. He had a knack for summarizing obscure theological points in short, pithy slogans. It's easy to see why Achillas might be impressed.

Achillas did not live long. He died in 312, after only six months in the bishop's chair.

And then, as Peter might have predicted, Arius advanced himself as the obvious candidate to be the next bishop of Alexandria. He had all the right qualities, after all: entertaining eloquence, cosmopolitan education, and broad support.

But his support wasn't quite broad enough. The clergy chose their native-born brother Alexander to succeed Achillas as bishop.

Alexander was, of course, the other man who had heard Peter's warning about Arius. So here was another chance to fix the problem. But Alexander, like Achillas before him, chose the path of conciliation and tried to win over Arius by benign neglect.

Arius would not be won over, but once again, he made the most of his bishop's leniency. He gathered about him an assortment of disciples, patrons, and flatterers. He had never suffered a deficit of confidence. But now he grew bolder.

He had contempt for Alexander, whom he considered his intellectual inferior. How could he have lost the election to such a man? Yet Arius would go to listen to Alexander preach. And there he would seethe with resentment. In the year 318, during one of these liturgies, Alexander was preaching at length about Jesus as the *eternal Son* of God the Father.

Arius could stand it no longer. He stood up in the midst of the congregation and denounced his bishop as a heretic.

Well, now the opposition was public. Now the rebellion was in the open. Alexander tried dialogue, and that failed. He hosted several conferences to settle the dispute, and they went nowhere. Arius just dug in, encouraged by his entourage.

Alexander wanted to be deliberate and act with justice. So he summoned a synod of a hundred bishops and put the problem before them. They decided overwhelmingly to excommunicate Arius and his followers.

A Crash Course in Arianism

What was the doctrine in dispute?

Arius was a man of hard logic. Today we would call him a rationalist. He said it was simply impossible for God the Father and God the Son to be coequal and coeternal. By definition, a father must precede his son in time. By nature, a son is subject to his father's authority and therefore inferior. Any talk of coequality and coeternity was nonsense to Arius.

He believed Jesus to be the greatest of creatures, the first of creatures — but a creature nonetheless, and certainly not the Creator. Jesus' sonship, according to Arius, was adoptive, not natural — and the term *Son of God* was really no more than an honorific metaphor.

Arius's special genius was not for theology but, rather, for advertising jingles. And so he reduced his doctrine to slogans, which he set to music. The most popular was a little sentence: "There was when he was not."

"There was when he was not."

It was so simple. It seemed so sensible.

"There was when he was not."

The phrase went viral. In Greek, it had a singsong rhythm like a nursery rhyme. It rolled off the tongue like a popular song.

And so Arius taught the world — wrongly — that there was a time before the Word of God existed. There was a time, then, when there was no divine Son. And so there was a time when God was not Father.

Alexander's rejection of this was visceral. The Church had worshiped Jesus as the eternal Word and the Son of God. The Church had always spoken of God as the eternal Father. Such was the divine mystery passed from Christ to his apostles. The Church had accepted it from the beginning, without quite comprehending it. Yet here was Arius turning the life of the Church topsy-turvy by denouncing Alexander as a heretic for praying as Christians had always prayed and teaching as

Christians had always taught.

By the year 318, the world itself had undergone an upheaval. The Roman Empire had been the Church's longstanding persecutor. But now, with the victory of Emperor Constantine, the empire had become the Church's defender and patron.

In the fourth century, there was no talk of separation between Church and state. So when Arius suffered excommunication in the city of Alexandria, he suffered banishment as well. He took to the road and found refuge with bishops who had been his classmates many years before in Antioch. Chief among his supporters was a man named Eusebius of Nicomedia, a bishop in Asia Minor who was quite influential at the imperial court. (Eusebius was a very common name in those days. We should be careful not to confuse Eusebius of Nicomedia with Eusebius of Caesarea, the historian, who was around at the same time.) Eusebius would make himself Arius's manager, so to speak. Most writers of the time saw Eusebius as a very ambitious man, and he certainly knew his way around imperial politics. It is hard to tell at this distance exactly what Eusebius believed, but it is easy to tell that he found in Arius a tool that he could use to push his way into more prominence and more power.

From his distant hideout, Arius continued to encourage dissent in Alexandria. He wrote a book called *The Banquet*, a mishmash of prose and poetry in which he responded to Alexander's condemnation and further developed his own subordinationist doctrine. The way he began it tells us a lot about how Arius saw himself:

> According to faith of God's elect, God's prudent ones,
> Holy children, rightly dividing, God's Holy Spirit receiving,
> Have I learned this from the partakers of wisdom,
> Accomplished, divinely taught, and wise in all things.
> Along their track have I been walking, with like opinions,
> I the very famous, the much suffering for God's glory;
> And taught of God, I have acquired wisdom and knowledge.[4]

Poor, old, very famous, much-suffering, wise, and knowing Arius! As Athanasius would later write, "Who can hear all this — who can even listen to the meter of the *Banquet* — without hating the way Arius jokes about these things as if he's on the stage?"[5]

Arius and his followers wrote to Alexander a statement of faith, in which they claimed that they held the faith of their forefathers and the faith they had also learned from Alexander:

> Our faith from our forefathers, which also we have learned from you, blessed Pope, is this: — We acknowledge One God, alone Ingenerate, alone Everlasting, alone Unoriginate, alone True, alone having Immortality, alone Wise, alone Good, alone Sovereign; Judge, Governor, and Providence of all, unalterable and unchangeable, just and good, God of Law and Prophets and New Testament; who generated an Only-begotten Son before eternal times, through whom He has made both the ages and the universe; and generated Him, not in semblance, but in truth; and that He made Him subsist at His own will unalterable and unchangeable; perfect creature of God, but not as one of the creatures. … For the Father did not, in giving to Him the inheritance of all things, deprive Himself, of what He has ingenerately in Himself; for He is the Fountain of all things.

Thus there are Three Subsistences. And God, being the cause of all things, is Unoriginate and altogether Sole, but the Son being generated apart from time by the Father, and being created and founded before ages, was not before His generation, but being generated apart from time before all things, alone was made to subsist by the Father. For he is not eternal or co-eternal or co-ingenerate with the Father, nor has he his being together with the Father, as some speak of relations, introducing two ingenerate origins, but God is before all things as being a One and an Origin of all. Wherefore also He is before the Son; as we have learned also from your preaching in the midst of the Church.[6]

Alexander's Response

Alexander was sure he had never said anything like that. He responded with letters of refutation. Apparently, he wrote many. He wrote to individual bishops. He wrote to the Church at large. And he wrote for the sake of his people in Alexandria. Only two of his letters have survived, one addressed to another bishop named Alexander, the other an encyclical letter addressed as a warning to Christians in general. In the latter, he summarizes the doctrines of Arius and his followers, and he lays out the consequences of that one little singsong slogan that Arius insisted on:

> And their unscriptural novelties are these: —
>
> "God was not always a Father, but once was not a Father.
>
> "The Word of God was not always existing, but came into being out of nothing; for God who is, did make out of nothing him who was not. Therefore once he was not, for the Son is a creature and work.
>
> "He is neither like in substance to the Father, nor the Father's true and natural Word; nor is He His true Wisdom; but He is one of those things which were made and brought to be, and only by an abuse of words, Word and Wisdom, having come into existence Himself by God's own Word and God's intrinsic Wisdom, by which God made all things, and Him in their number.
>
> "Accordingly He, the Word of God, is by nature mutable and variable, as are all rational beings; and foreign and alien and separated off from the substance of God.

"And to the Son the Father is an ineffable God, for not properly and accurately does the Son know the Father, nor can He perfectly see Him. For neither does the Son know His own substance, as it really is; for He was made for our sake, in order that by Him, as by an instrument, God might create us; and He would not have subsisted, unless God had wished to create us."

Accordingly, when they were asked whether the Word of God could change, as the devil had changed, they were not afraid to answer, "Yes, He can; for having come into being by creation, He is of a mutable nature."

Alexander's replies to these assertions are blunt and clear. He says in no uncertain terms that this is the true apostolic faith:

That the Word is eternal and not created.
That the Word became flesh in Jesus Christ.
That Jesus is true God.
That Jesus is one in being with the Father.

Concerning him we thus believe, even as the Apostolic Church believes. In one Father unbegotten, who has from no one the cause of His being, who is unchangeable and immutable, who is always the same, and admits of no increase or diminution; who gave us the Law, the prophets, and the Gospels; who is Lord of the patriarchs and apostles, and all the saints. And in one Lord Jesus Christ, the only begotten Son of God; not begotten of things which are not, but of Him who is the Father.

Alexander's response was effective, but so were the relentless efforts of Arius in his exile. Both sides gathered passionate supporters and advocates. The argument divided parishes into factions and placed Christians in every land squarely in opposition to their bishops.

Constantine Intervenes

By the year 324, the Church in the East had taken on the qualities of a dumpster fire. And in July of that year, when Emperor Constantine laid claim to that half of the empire, he found it to be a shambles. The ecclesiastical dispute over Arianism posed the gravest threat to imperial unity. How was Constantine going to keep the barbarians at bay if he could not unite his own subjects — if his own subjects, in fact, were on the brink of war with one another?

At first, he wrote a letter to Arius and Alexander, telling them how sad he was that Alexandria should be torn by strife between Christians:

> And yet, having made a careful inquiry into the origin and foundation of these differences, I find the cause to be of a truly insignificant character, and quite unworthy of such fierce contention. Feeling myself, therefore, compelled to address you in this letter, and to appeal at the same time to your unanimity and sagacity, I call on Divine Providence to assist me in the task, while I interrupt your dissension in the character of a minister of peace.

To Constantine, who had a soldier's impatience with subtlety, it seemed that Alexander and Arius were equally to blame.

> I understand, then, that the occasion of your present controversy is to be traced to the following circumstances; that you, Alexander, demanded of the priests what opinion they each held respecting a certain passage in the Divine law, or

> rather, I should say, that you asked them some-
> thing connected with an unprofitable question;
> and then that you, Arius, inconsiderately gave ut-
> terance to objections which ought never to have
> been conceived at all, or if conceived, should
> have been buried in profound silence.

The problem, as Constantine saw it, was that the clergy
had too much time on their hands. They were arguing
about useless questions, and they should just realize that
some questions are too hard to bother with.

> Now therefore, both of you, bear with me a lit-
> tle, and take the advice that your fellow-servant
> feels himself justly entitled to give. What then
> is this advice? It was wrong in the first instance
> to propose such questions as these, or to reply
> to them when they were brought up. For those
> points of discussion which are enjoined by the
> authority of no law, but rather suggested by the
> contentious spirit which is fostered by misused
> leisure, even though they may be intended
> merely as an intellectual exercise, ought cer-
> tainly to be confined to the region of our own
> thoughts, and neither hastily produced in the

public assemblies of the saints, nor unadvisedly entrusted to the general ear. …

So let both the unguarded question and the inconsiderate answer receive your mutual forgiveness. Your difference has not arisen on any leading doctrines or precepts of the Divine law, nor have you introduced any new dogma respecting the worship of God. You are in truth of one and the same judgment: you may therefore well join in that communion which is the symbol of united fellowship.[7]

It was a very nice letter. Can't we all just get along? And the answer, of course, was no. Constantine had missed what Alexander — and his right-hand man, Athanasius — saw as the very crux of the controversy, so to speak. If Christ is not God, then salvation can't happen. We should remember that Constantine was a Latin speaker who was not completely comfortable with Greek, the language in which the whole controversy was being carried on so far. When he "made a careful inquiry into the origin and foundation of these differences," he probably had to rely on what people close to him told him about the issues. People close to emperors tend to tell the emperor what they think he wants to hear, and Constantine very much wanted to hear that this little difficulty could be smoothed over without much effort.

Eusebius of Caesarea, the historian, was an un-abashed fan of Constantine, but from the way he describes the situation after the letter, we might guess that even he thought Constantine was a bit naive. "The evil, however, was greater than could be remedied by a single letter, so that the bitterness of the contending parties continually increased, and the effects of the mischief extended to all the Eastern provinces. Such were the fruits of the jealousy of that evil spirit who looked with an envious eye on the prosperity of the Church."[8]

Constantine was a very tolerant man as far as religion went. What he didn't like was disorder. The Roman Empire had had entirely too much disorder before he came to power, but he had sorted most of it out. This dispute in the Church was causing riots and constant arguments. It needed to be sorted out.

Constantine Calls a Council

So Constantine did something unprecedented. He convoked a synod of the world's bishops — an *ecumenical* council, meaning a council of the whole Church — to meet in 325 in Nicaea, one of the suburbs of his brand-new imperial capital New Rome (later to be known as Constantinople):

> Nor was this merely the issuing of a bare com-
> mand, but the emperor's condescension con-
> tributed much to its being carried into effect:
> for he allowed some the use of the public means
> of conveyance, while he afforded others an am-
> ple supply of horses for their transport. The
> place, too, selected for the synod, the city Nicaea
> in Bithynia (which derived its name from Nike,
> "Victory") was appropriate to the occasion.

Bishops brought large retinues with them. Constantine
was paying for it, after all. Eusebius tells us that "the
number of priests and deacons in their train, and the
crowd of acolytes and other attendants, was completely
beyond calculation."[9]

One of those deacons was Alexander's right-hand
man, Athanasius.

More than three hundred bishops accepted the
summons. Many of them were old men who had suffered torture for the Faith during the years of persecution. Eyewitnesses reported that Constantine kissed
their wounds as they entered the council chambers.

There had been local assemblies of bishops before.

But this was the first assembly of the whole Church, and it was the first time the bishops had gathered under the authority of an emperor. And though the emperor was very respectful to the bishops, Constantine's stage management of the occasion left no one in any doubt about who was emperor around here:

> And now, all rising at the signal which indicated the emperor's entrance, at last he himself proceeded through the midst of the assembly, like some heavenly messenger of God, clothed in raiment which glittered as it were with rays of light, reflecting the glowing radiance of a purple robe, and adorned with the brilliant splendor of gold and precious stones. Such was the external appearance of his person; and with regard to his mind, it was evident that he was distinguished by piety and godly fear. This was indicated by his downcast eyes, the blush on his countenance, and the modesty of his gait.

The emperor himself addressed the assembled bishops — in Latin, since he was a Westerner, with an interpreter to translate his words into Greek. He reminded them of how fortunate they had been to be delivered (by Constantine) from the tyrants and persecutors of the past, and he told them how much it meant to him to have peace and harmony in the Christian Church:

> And now I rejoice in seeing your assembly; but I feel that my desires will be most completely fulfilled when I can see you all united in one judgment, and that common spirit of peace and concord prevailing amongst you all, which it becomes you, as consecrated to the service of God, to commend to others. Do not delay, then, dear friends. Do not delay, ministers of God, and faithful servants of Him who is our common Lord and Savior. Begin from this moment to discard the causes of that disunion which has existed among you, and remove the perplexities of controversy by embracing the principles of peace. For by such conduct you will at the same time be acting in a manner most pleasing to the supreme God, and you will confer an exceeding favor on me who am your fellow-servant.[10]

Then the circus began. "As soon as the emperor had spoken these words in the Latin tongue, which another present rendered into Greek, he gave permission to those who presided in the council to deliver their opinions. On this some began to accuse their neighbours, who defended themselves, and recriminated in their turn. In this manner numberless assertions were put forth by each party, and a violent controversy arose at the very beginning."[11]

Later legends (and some historians defend them as preserving true history) tell us that the controversy became so violent that one of the bishops slapped Arius across the face. That bishop was St. Nicholas of Myra, more familiar as the red-coated gentleman who brings toys to good little boys and girls at Christmas. Santa Claus has a more interesting origin story than most people realize.

The historian Sozomen tells us that the council was a good opportunity for the bishops to display their rhetorical skill. But it turned out that the one who dominated the discussion wasn't a bishop at all:

> As might have been expected, however, many different questions started out of the investigation: some of the bishops spoke against the introduction of novelties contrary to the faith which had been delivered to them from the beginning. And the ones who stood up for simplicity of doctrine

argued that the faith of God ought to be received without curious inquiries; others, however, contended that ancient opinions ought not to be followed without examination. Many of the bishops who were then assembled, and of the clergy who accompanied them, being remarkable for their skill in debate, and practiced in such rhetorical methods, became conspicuous, and attracted the notice of the emperor and the court. Of that number Athanasius, who was then a deacon of Alexandria, and had accompanied his bishop Alexander, seemed to have the largest share in the counsel concerning these subjects.[12]

As the debates went on, young Athanasius became more and more conspicuous. He seemed to dominate the discussion. He had a way of drilling down to the essentials that made him very hard to refute. Naturally, he was making plenty of enemies among the people who couldn't overcome his arguments.

The council was not entirely about the Arian controversy. Constantine wanted the bishops to resolve all other disputes and divisions, as long as they were sequestered in his outbuildings. Another agenda item was the celebration of Easter. Some churches observed the feast on the anniversary date of the Resurrection, while others kept the feast on a proximate Sunday. The council also turned its attention to the long-lasting schism of Melitius of Lycopolis and his Church of the Martyrs.

Constantine moderated the debate, "according to his understanding of what he heard, for he was not wholly unpracticed in the Greek language," as Sozomen says.[13] We can imagine that his imperfect Greek was taxed to the limit by the arguments he had to sit through.

Yet in spite of the loud arguments, Arius really had very little support. Sozomen tells us that, at the beginning, there were only seventeen at the council who "praised the opinion of Arius." Most of them changed their minds later on. So, out of more than three hundred bishops, there were ultimately fewer than seventeen Arians.

The Result of the Council

At last, the council came to its conclusion: "They affirmed the Son to be consubstantial with the Father; and that those are to be excommunicated and voted aliens to the Catholic Church, who assert that there was a time in which the Son existed not, and before He was begotten He was not, and that He was made from what had no existence, and that He is of another hypostasis or substance from the Father, and that He is subject to change or mutation."[14] Among the bishops who signed their names to that decision was Eusebius of Nicomedia.

In order to make it clear exactly what the council had decided, a statement of belief was published:

> We believe in one God, the Father Almighty,
> Maker of all things, visible and invisible:
> And in one Lord Jesus Christ, the Son of God,
> begotten of the Father, only begotten, that is, of
>   the substance of the Father;
> God from God; Light from light; true God from
>   true God; begotten, not made; being con-
>   substantial with the Father,
> By whom all things were made, both things in
>   heaven and things in earth:
> Who for us men and for our salvation came
>   down, and was incarnate, and was made
>   man:
> He suffered, and rose again the third day:
>   And ascended into heaven:
> And shall come again to judge the living and the
>   dead.
> And in the Holy Spirit, etc.[†]

[†]The "etc." is not in the original, but it seems obvious that the original creed, repeating earlier local creeds, included more of the text we use today. See the statement of faith of Arius later.

This should sound very familiar to most Christians today. With some additions from a later ecumenical council, this is the statement of belief we still use today — the one we call the Nicene Creed, named for the Council of Nicaea.

That word *consubstantial* — in Greek, *homoousios* — was the key to the council's decrees. It means having the same being or essence. The Son is of the same essence as the Father. This was exactly what the Arians could not accept, and therefore it was exactly the thing the council had to insist on.

The anti-Arius side had won. No big surprise, since there were so few bishops who agreed with Arius even before the debate started.

Well, that settled it. Constantine was pleased. Everything could go back to normal.

By Constantine's decree, Arius was exiled. He was not allowed to return to Alexandria. His works, including *The Banquet*, were banned, with the death penalty for secretly keeping them.

Meanwhile, the council also tried to solve the problem of the Melitians. Melitius himself would be able to keep the title of bishop, but he was not allowed to perform any ordinations.

So, in every dispute, the assembled bishops had adopted the position of Alexander of Alexandria as their own — that is, as the official position of the Catholic Church. Alexander triumphed in every debate — or, rather, his deacon Athanasius triumphed in the debates by stating Alexander's position with such force that no one could deny it. Alexander emerged as the acknowledged victor, not only in the Arian controversy but in at least two other major quarrels.

From our viewpoint seventeen centuries later, it looks as if Alexander pitched a perfect game. He should have returned to Alexandria in triumph, carried on the shoulders of his team.

But reality was much messier. Today, we're fairly comfortable with the idea of an ecumenical council. But in 325, it was a novelty, an innovation introduced by an unbaptized emperor. Not everyone was willing to acknowledge its authority or respect its decisions.

The sad truth is that Alexander still had to fight the fight against Arius. His successors would still be fighting it seventy-five years later. And the parallel church of Melitius would continue to operate, guerilla style, in the Egyptian countryside. Meanwhile, in the imperial court, Eusebius of Nicomedia was seething with resentment. He had not been able to avoid signing the majority opinion of the council, but he was unhappy about the exile of his friend and useful puppet Arius. He was planning his revenge.

Alexander died in 328, just three years after the council. He had served as bishop for sixteen years. Of his life during those years we know very little. We have just a couple of his writings, some fragments of his homilies, and precious few anecdotes from his contemporaries. Almost all we know of his life is that it collided with the life of Arius. Alexander is remembered with honor because he was the *first* man to enter dread combat with history's most notorious heretic.

In his lifetime, Alexander never saw matters settled, but he surely saw hope for the future of his Church. His hope was embodied in the person of his chief lieutenant and personally designated successor: the deacon Athanasius.

3.
The Young Bishop

Some sources say that, as he was dying, old Bishop Alexander made clear his wish to have Athanasius as his successor. And the clergy honored that wish.

Athanasius was still very young. In fact, his opponents would sometimes claim that he had not yet reached the minimum canonical age of thirty. Since the charge was repeated, it must have seemed credible.

Athanasius was young, but he was likely optimistic about his prospects. Since the council had ruled in favor of the full divinity of Christ, he had the bishops of the world on his side. And the emperor himself had given the council decrees legal teeth.

But Athanasius had made powerful enemies. They immediately began plotting to get rid of him.

One of their first attempts was to accuse him of having conspired in a plot against Constantine. According to the historian Theodoret, they had bribed some witnesses. The charges were brought to the emperor, but he dismissed them. "Believe me, my brethren," he wrote to the people of Alexandria, "the wicked were unable to accomplish anything against your bishop. … I joyfully welcomed Athanasius your bishop; and I have conversed with him as with one whom I know to be a man of God."[1]

So far, Athanasius had the emperor on his side, and that was certainly a big advantage. But that only meant that his opponents would have to try harder.

Constantine Softens

Meanwhile, Constantine was beginning to have a change of heart about the Arians. Arius's allies — especially Eusebius of Nicomedia, who always seemed to be wherever the emperor was — were lobbying for a generous toleration of dissent, and eventually they prevailed. Constantine relaxed his Arian laws. In 333, Arius was summoned to court, and he made a profession of faith that satisfied Constantine:

> In accordance with the command of your devout piety, sovereign lord, we declare our faith, and before God profess in writing, that we and our adherents believe as follows:
>
> "We believe in one God the Father Almighty: and in the Lord Jesus Christ his Son, who was begotten of him before all ages, God the Word through whom all things were made, both those which are in the heavens and those upon the earth; who descended, and became incarnate, and suffered, and rose again, ascended into the heavens, and will again come to judge the living and the dead. Also in the Holy Spirit, and in the resurrection of the flesh, and in the life of the coming age, and in the kingdom of the heavens, and in one Catholic Church of God, extending from one end of the earth to the other."[2]
>
> This faith we have received from the holy gospels, where the Lord says to his disciples: "Go therefore and make disciples of all nations, baptizing them in the name of the Father and of

the Son and of the Holy Spirit" (Mt 28:19). If we do not so believe and truly receive the Father, the Son, and the Holy Spirit, as the whole Catholic Church and the holy Scriptures teach (in which we believe in every respect), God is our judge both now, and in the coming judgment. Wherefore we beseech your piety, most devout emperor, that we who are persons consecrated to the ministry, and holding the faith and sentiments of the church and of the holy Scriptures, may by your pacific and devoted piety be reunited to our mother, the Church, all superfluous questions and disputes being avoided: that so both we and the whole church being at peace, may in common offer our accustomed prayers for your tranquil reign, and on behalf of your whole family.[3]

This sounded very good. Only someone who was really paying attention might have noticed that Arius avoided using the word *consubstantial* and that he specifically avoided mentioning what the "superfluous questions and disputes" were — meaning that there were still some things he wouldn't agree to, but, hey, they weren't very important.

So Arius was allowed to return from exile.

But Athanasius made it clear that he would *not* be welcome in Alexandria or anywhere in Egypt or Libya, all of which was under Alexandrian authority. Athanasius adamantly refused to lift Arius's excommunication. He was unimpressed by the emperor's change of heart. And Athanasius remained unswayed as one bishop after another moved to conform to the new imperial policy of tolerance.

Many of the bishops began to resent Athanasius's seemingly eccentric resistance to Constantine's newer laws regarding Arianism. All the bishops were loosening up. Why did Athanasius — the bishop in such an influential church — have to be different? Why couldn't he just go along to get along? They interpreted his resistance as an unspoken reproach, and they resented it.

From the beginning, then, we can see the firmness, steadfastness, obstinacy, and stubbornness that would characterize his life thereafter. He was not there to make friends or to get along with others. He was heir to the teaching office of the apostles, and he would be faithful to that office and its inheritance — no matter the cost.

Here's how he described his duty in a letter to another bishop, a fellow Egyptian named Serapion: "In accordance with the apostolic faith delivered to us by tradition from the Fathers, I have delivered the tradition, without inventing anything extraneous to it. What I learned, that have I inscribed conformably with the holy Scriptures; for it also conforms with those passages from the holy Scriptures which we have cited above by way of proof."

He urged Serapion to "look at the very tradition, teaching, and faith of the Catholic Church from the very beginning … which the Lord gave, the Apostles preached, and the Fathers kept. Upon this the Church is founded, and he who should fall away from it would not be a Christian, and should no longer be so called."[4]

Athanasius was a man certain of his principles, and he was not about to back away — though the personal cost would be dear. The plots against him became more and more extravagant. They would have been silly if they had not also been dangerous.

"The calumniators of Athanasius felt no remorse," says Theodoret; "on the contrary, they devised so bold a fiction against him, that it surpassed any fable that had been invented by the ancient writers, whether comic or tragic."[5] This time, according to Theodoret, the bribed witnesses included some bishops who were Arian sympathizers. Of course, Eusebius of Nicomedia was in on the plot — or at least he seized on the charges as a way to get back at Athanasius.

What were the charges? We can't tell you, said the enemies of Athanasius. That's how horrible they are. He needs to be tried and dethroned by a council of his peers. "The emperor little suspected that bishops could be capable of such duplicity, and was perfectly ignorant of their intrigues," says Theodoret. "He was, therefore, persuaded by them to act as they desired."[6]

The Synod of Tyre

Constantine gave his authority to the synod. He wrote a letter full of his usual confidence that things could be sorted out quickly because, of course, Christian bishops will be above reproach:

> Constantine Augustus to the holy council assembled in Tyre.
>
> In the general prosperity which distinguishes the present time, it seems right that the Catholic Church should likewise be exempt from trouble, and that the servants of Christ should be freed from every reproach.
>
> But certain individuals instigated by the mad desire of contention, not to say leading a life unworthy of their profession, are endeavoring to

throw all into disorder. This appears to me to be the greatest of all possible calamities. I beseech you, therefore, to assemble together posthaste, as the saying goes, without any delay, in formal synod; so that you may support those who require your assistance, heal the brethren who are in danger, restore unanimity to the divided members, and rectify the disorders of the Church while time permits; and thus restore to those great provinces the harmony which, alas! the arrogance of a few men has destroyed. I believe every one would admit that you could not perform anything so pleasing in the sight of God, so surpassing all my prayers as well as your own, or so conducive to your own reputation, as to restore peace.

All that now devolves upon your holinesses is to decide with unanimous judgment, without partiality or prejudice, in accordance with the ecclesiastical and apostolical rule, and to devise suitable remedies for the offences which may have resulted from error; in order that the Church may be freed from all reproach, that my anxiety may be diminished, that peace may be restored to those now at variance, and that your renown may be increased. May God preserve you, beloved brethren.[7]

So Athanasius was forced to defend himself at a synod in Tyre, and there he faced the charges against him — which were horrible indeed:

> Arsenius was the bishop of the Melitian faction. His partisans put him in hiding, and requested him to remain there. They then cut off the right hand of a corpse, embalmed it, placed it in a wooden coffin, and carried it about everywhere, declaring that it was the hand of Arsenius, who had been murdered by Athanasius.[8]

Supposedly Athanasius had murdered Arsenius and cut off his hand to use in some fiendish magic ritual. There were other charges as well. The prosecution brought in "a woman of loose principles." She had a horrible charge to make, too: She had vowed perpetual virginity, but Athanasius had raped her when he was staying in her house.

Fortunately, Athanasius had friends who were willing to lend him a bit of help, and they had already done some slick detective work. The council devolved into a *Perry Mason* courtroom drama. When the woman of loose principles came into the chamber and made her accusation, Athanasius ignored her. Instead, a priest named Timotheus turned to her and said, "Have I ever even spoken with you or entered your house?"

> She replied with the utmost effrontery, railed at Timotheus, and, pointing at him with her finger, she exclaimed, "You are the one who committed the act of violence against me!" And she added other indelicate expressions which are used by women destitute of all modesty.

Well, that was embarrassing for the prosecution. Those charges were dropped.

> Athanasius said that instead of sending her away they ought to find out from her the names of those by whom she had been employed; but his accusers replied that he had perpetrated other flagrant crimes, of which it was utterly impossible that he could by any art be exonerated; and that eyes, even without ears, were sufficient to demonstrate his culpability. Having said this, they exhibited the famous coffin, and exposed the embalmed hand to view.

This created consternation in the court. Some people were convinced. Some thought it must be a trick. There was a lot of uproar, and it took a while for silence to be restored. But Athanasius was strangely calm through it all.

When the noise died down at last, Athanasius asked the people present whether any of them knew Arsenius. Several of them replied that they had known him very well.

Immediately there was a stir at the entrance, and some of Athanasius's friends brought a man into the chamber, his arms covered by his cloak.

"Is this the Arsenius who lost a hand?" Athanasius asked.

The people who knew him immediately recognized him: it was indeed Arsenius, and he was definitely alive.

Athanasius took hold of the man's sleeves and lifted them up, showing two intact hands.

"Arsenius seems to have two hands," Athanasius told the assembly. "Let my accusers show you where the third one was cut off."

This produced a bigger uproar than before. Some shouted that Athanasius had used sorcery to deceive their eyes. But the murder charge could not stick.[9]

The council was determined to find *something* to

convict Athanasius of, though, so it finally settled on a story that may or may not be true but has little to do with Athanasius himself. A man named Ischyras had claimed to be a priest without being ordained. Athanasius had sent someone named Macarius to stop Ischyras from saying Mass, and Ischyras claimed that Macarius had overturned the altar, broken the sacred vessels, and burned the Scriptures.

Athanasius demanded an investigation of the facts, and the council appointed a committee of Athanasius's accusers to investigate. This hardly seemed reasonable, and Athanasius said so. But the shouting against him was starting to turn into physical violence, until the guards who had been sent by the emperor to keep order slipped him out of the hall secretly, fearing for his life. They were afraid Athanasius was going to be murdered by a gathering of bishops.

The investigators, meanwhile, went off to Egypt, where they refused to allow any eyewitnesses to speak to them. Instead, they interviewed the people who had made the accusations, and they came back with the report that Macarius was definitely guilty of having desecrated sacred vessels.

So the absent Athanasius was convicted of having been bishop when Macarius did that, and he was deposed as bishop of Alexandria.

Meanwhile, the council convened again at Jerusalem and readmitted Arius to communion, showing that the charges against Athanasius were really about Arius, not about magic, murder, rape, and desecration.

Athanasius Appeals to Constantine

Athanasius had already shown himself "a master of what may be called, without disrespect, theatrical effect," in the words of one nineteenth-century historian.[10] He decided on one last desperate theatrical gesture. He went to Constantinople and waited by the side of the road until Constantine came by; then he stopped the emperor and demanded a trial in which he could face his accusers in the emperor's presence. Constantine was fair-minded enough to see the justice in that, so he granted Athanasius's request.

But it didn't go well for Athanasius. None of the charges of murder or rape were brought up this time — not even the Macarius incident. Instead, Athanasius's enemies had a new accusation, and one that showed they probably had got some good advice about what would really worry the emperor. We sense the intervention of Eusebius of Nicomedia, who knew very well what would bother Constantine the most. Athanasius was charged

with threatening to stop the grain shipments from Alexandria if the emperor didn't bow to his wishes.

This was a big deal. Constantinople had already
become a huge city, and all its grain came from Egypt.
(The city of Rome was in a similar position: It got all
its grain from Africa, meaning the part that is now Al-
geria, Tunisia, and Morocco.) There had already been
food problems when unfavorable winds had delayed the
shipments, and the mob in the city had accused a pagan
philosopher named Sopater of holding back the winds
with his magic. Riots were beginning. Even though he
was a personal friend of Constantine, Sopater had to die
to quell the mob, just because the wind was from the
wrong direction. The one thing you didn't mess with
was Constantinople's grain supply.

A letter from the Egyptian bishops told what happened, citing eyewitness reports:

> Certain of our friends were present at the pal-
> ace with Athanasius, and heard the threats of
> the Emperor upon receiving this report. And
> when Athanasius cried out upon the calumny,
> and positively declared that it was not true (for
> how, he argued, should he a poor man, and in
> a private station, be able to do such a thing?),

Eusebius [of Nicomedia] did not hesitate publicly to repeat the charge, and swore that Athanasius was a rich man, and powerful, and able to do anything; in order that it might be supposed from these things that he had used this language. Such was the accusation these venerable Bishops proffered against him. But the grace of God proved superior to their wickedness, for it moved the pious Emperor to mercy, who instead of death passed upon him the sentence of banishment. Thus their calumnies, and nothing else, were the cause of this.[11]

This time they got Athanasius — but they didn't get him killed. The emperor was alarmed, and he exiled Athanasius to the far west, to the cold, distant territory today known as Germany.

This would be Exile Number One.

4.
Constantius Takes Over

The purpose of exile was to render the offender ineffective — to punish him by removing him from the advantages of his home and to silence his voice in the cities that mattered. Almost all of those cities were in the eastern regions of the empire. Sending Athanasius way out west was supposed to put him out of the way and silence his nagging voice.

Well, it didn't work.

Athanasius could have spent his exile pouting and lamenting. But he didn't. He used his years abroad — as

Arius had done earlier   to make new friends and allies and extend his influence.

Meanwhile, strangely, Athanasius was still bishop of Alexandria. No successor was appointed. Constantine seems to have been a little ambivalent about Athanasius, and in fact — as we'll soon see — Constantine's son would later claim that the blessed Constantine had sent Athanasius away for his own good.

The Sudden End of Arius

Athanasius's exile was a triumph for the Arians, especially Eusebius of Nicomedia. But Arius didn't have long to enjoy it. Just as he was really getting back on top of things, he suddenly died — on the toilet — at the worst possible moment for his cause. Athanasius tells the story in a letter he wrote to his fellow bishop Serapion:

> I was not at Constantinople when he died, but Macarius the Priest was, and I heard the account of it from him.
>
> Arius had been invited by the Emperor Constantine, through the intervention of Eusebius [of Nicomedia] and his fellows; and when he entered the presence the Emperor asked him whether he held the faith of the Catholic

Church. And he declared upon oath that he held the right faith, and gave an account of his faith in writing, suppressing the points for which he had been cast out of the Church by Bishop Alexander, and speciously alleging expressions out of the Scriptures.

When therefore he swore that he did not profess the opinions for which Alexander had excommunicated him, [the emperor] dismissed him, saying, "If your faith is right, you have done well to swear. But if you have sworn even though your faith is impious, God judge you according to your oath."

When he thus came forth from the presence of the Emperor, Eusebius and his fellows, with their usual violence, desired to bring him into the Church. But Alexander, the Bishop of Constantinople of blessed memory, resisted them, saying that the inventor of the heresy ought not to be admitted to communion; whereupon Eusebius and his fellows threatened, declaring, "As we have caused him to be invited by the Emperor, in opposition to your wishes, so tomorrow, though it be contrary to your desire, Arius shall have communion with us in this Church." It was the Sabbath when they said this.

When Bishop Alexander heard this, he was greatly distressed, and entering into the church, he stretched forth his hands unto God, and bewailed himself; and casting himself upon his face in the chancel, he prayed, lying upon the pavement. Macarius also was present, and prayed with him, and heard his words. And he besought these two things, saying, "If Arius is brought to communion tomorrow, let me, your servant, depart, and do not destroy the pious with the impious; but if you will spare your Church (and I know that you will spare), look upon the words of Eusebius and his fellows, and do not hand over your inheritance to destruction and reproach, and take away Arius — otherwise, if he enters the Church, the heresy also might seem to enter with him, and henceforward impiety be taken for piety."

When the Bishop had thus prayed, he retired in great anxiety. And a wonderful and extraordinary thing happened. While Eusebius and his fellows were making threats, the Bishop was praying; but Arius, who had great confidence in Eusebius and his fellows, and was talking very wildly, withdrew to answer the call of nature, and suddenly, in the language of Scripture, "falling headlong he burst open in the middle,"* and immediately expired as he lay, and was deprived both of communion and of his life together.

That is how Arius met his end: and Eusebius and his fellows, overwhelmed with shame, buried their accomplice, while the blessed Alexander, amidst the rejoicings of the Church, celebrated the Communion with piety and orthodoxy, praying with all the brethren, and greatly glorifying God. Not that he was exulting in his death (God forbid!), for "it is appointed for men to die once" (Heb 9:27), but because this thing had been shown forth in a manner transcending human judgments. For the Lord Himself, judging between the threats of Eusebius and his fellows and the prayer of Alexander, condemned the Arian heresy, showing it to be unworthy of communion with the Church, and making it obvious to all, that even if it has the support of the Emperor and of all mankind, yet it was condemned by the Church herself.

---

*The description of Judas's end in Acts 1:18.

So the antichristian gang of the Arian madmen has been shown to be unpleasing to God
and impious; and many of those who before
were deceived by it changed their opinions. For
none other than the Lord Himself who was blas-
phemed by them condemned the heresy which
rose up against Him, and again shewed that
howsoever the Emperor Constantius may now
use violence to the Bishops in behalf of it, yet it
is excluded from the communion of the Church,
and alien from the kingdom of heaven.[1]

You might expect that the death of their leader would
be a blow to the whole Arian sect. But it hardly made a
difference. That was probably because Arius had long
since ceased to be the real leader. It was Eusebius of
Nicomedia who pulled the strings, and he could think
on his feet. Losing his figurehead might be a temporary
inconvenience, but Eusebius had the sharp wit and the
political connections to recover and go on to more and
more influence.

So, though Arius died just a year after Athanasius
was exiled, his heresy continued unabated, promoted
now by Eusebius of Nicomedia and his followers. Arianism was probably stronger, in fact, with Arius gone.

His followers were softening his language, moderating his claims, and mutating his heresy in several ways. As the years wore on, Arianism would become a phenomenon increasingly difficult to define. There were just too many variations on the theme.

One clever variation was an *iota.*

Iota is the smallest letter in the Greek alphabet. It's proverbially insignificant. "For truly, I say to you, till heaven and earth pass away, not an iota, not a dot, will pass from the law until all is accomplished," said Jesus in the Sermon on the Mount (see Mt 5:18). (He was probably referring to the Hebrew letter *yodh*, which is the smallest letter in the Hebrew alphabet.) Our English word *jot*, as in "not one jot," comes from *iota.*

Now, the thing the Arians couldn't stomach in the Nicene definition of the Faith was that word *homoousios* — "consubstantial" or "of the same substance." But just add an *iota* to it, and it becomes *homoiousios* — "of *similar* substance." We can all agree on that, right? It's hardly different at all. Just add an *iota*, and stop being so stubborn.

As long as the saintly old Alexander was bishop of Constantinople, though, the Eusebians — as Athanasius would often call them — did not dare make any overt moves. Alexander was very popular, and it was just possible that Eusebius and his friends would have to think twice about going to the bathroom if they crossed him.

But Alexander was also ancient. He died not long after at the age of ninety-eight. He recommended his deacon Paul to succeed him, and the clergy of Constantinople took his recommendation. Paul was a good preacher and was staunchly orthodox. But he would not turn out to be very skilled at dealing with imperial politics.

Constantine's Sons

The death of Arius was followed within a year by the death of the emperor Constantine in 337.

The event brought some good news for Athanasius. Constantine, in his will, had divided governance of the empire among his three sons. Two of those sons, Constantine II and Constans, were sympathetically disposed to Athanasius and the Nicene faith.

Constantine II almost immediately sent Athanasius back to Alexandria, with a letter to the Alexandrians explaining that Athanasius had really been sent to Gaul for his own protection:

> You cannot, I believe, be unacquainted with the fact that Athanasius, the interpreter of the venerated law, since the cruelty of his bloodthirsty

and hostile enemies continued, to the danger of his sacred person, was sent for a time into Gaul in order that he might not incur irretrievable extremities through the perversity of these worthless opponents. In order then to make this danger futile, he was taken out of the jaws of the men, who pressed upon him, and was commanded to live near me, so that in the city where he dwelt, he might be amply furnished with all necessaries. But his virtue is so famous and extraordinary, because he is confident of Divine aid, that he thinks nothing of all the rougher burdens of fortune.

Our lord and my father, Constantine Augustus, of blessed memory, intended to have reinstated this bishop in his own place, and thus especially to have restored him to your much beloved piety; but, since he was anticipated by the human lot, and died before fulfilling his intention, I, as his successor, intend to carry into execution the design of the emperor of divine memory. Athanasius will inform you, when he sees your face, in how great reverence he was held by me. Nor is it surprising that I should have acted as I have done towards him, for the

image of your own desire and the appearance of
so noble a man, moved and impelled me to this
step. May Divine Providence watch over you,
my beloved brethren.[2]

Was Constantine telling the truth about his father's mo-
tivations? At this distance, we can't know for sure. While
Constantine was alive, he more than once complained
about that troublemaking Athanasius, so it's most likely
that his son was indulging in a polite fiction.

Constans and Constantine II soon had a falling out,
and Constantine II ended up dead. But Constans also
would always be friendly to Athanasius.

Constantius the Busybody

The bad news was all about the third son of Constantine. His name was Constantius, and he was inclined to
Arianism. And he was ruler over Athanasius's part of
the world. Constantius had just turned twenty a month
before his father died, and he would rule for the next
twenty-four years. He would eventually outlive and pre-
vail over his brother Constans, emerging in 350 as sole
ruler of the empire.

As soon as Constantius was established as ruler in
the East, he got his reign off on the right foot by mur-

dering all his relatives. Everyone who had a claim to be related to his great father, and thus was a potential threat to Constantius, was suddenly guilty of treason for one reason or another. The only ones spared were two cousins who were little boys at the time — Gallus and Julian.

Constantius was more of an intellectual — or perhaps pseudo-intellectual — than his father. He was very much interested in Christian theology, and as his reign went on, he would be more and more obsessed with making all the Christian bishops conform to his own Arian-leaning views.

This isn't just the verdict of Catholic historians, by the way. Ammianus Marcellinus was a pagan historian — one of the few pagan holdouts who didn't hate Christians. He thought that Christianity, as the apostles had taught it, was reasonable enough. But he couldn't understand all this squabbling over details in what was supposed to be a simple and straightforward religion. And squabbling over details was what Constantius liked best in the world.

He mixed up the plain and simple Christian religion with superstitious old wives' tales, and by making issues more complicated, instead of se-

> riously trying to settle them, he stirred up many
> divisions. As they spread, he fed them by wran-
> gling with words, so that, what with hordes of
> bishops running this way and that on the public
> transports to "synods," as they call them, while
> he was trying to drag the whole religion over to
> his own opinions, he hamstrung the transport
> system.[3]

Ammianus wasn't kidding about the synods. In 341,
there was a council at Antioch; in 342, one at Serdica.
In 345, there was a synod at Milan. In 347, there was a
council at Sirmium. In 351, there was another council at
Sirmium. In 353, Constantius made the bishops at the
synod of Arles condemn Athanasius; in 355, there was
a synod at Milan; in 357, a synod at Sirmium; in 358, a
synod at Ancyra and another one at Sirmium; in 359,
councils at Rimini and Seleucia; in 360, a synod at Constantinople. In 361, Constantius died at the age of for-
ty-four; otherwise, he would doubtless have continued
to pursue his favorite hobby.

You might think Ammianus was just being sarcastic
about the transport system, but he was probably quite
serious. Each time bishops were summoned to a synod,
they had the right to use the public transport system to

get where they were going. That transport system was meant for government affairs; it was one of the things that kept the imperial government running smoothly over such a vast territory. It included stables of draft animals, carriages, and public inns where the travelers could stay overnight and get a good meal. Early in his reign, Constantine had established the rule that bishops on official business had access to it too. And they had the right to bring all their retinue with them at no cost: secretaries, cooks, servants, and all manner of ecclesiastical bureaucrats who might be useful — and why not bring them if it's free?

In Constantine's reign, the privilege wasn't much of a burden on the government. But a council of the Church might potentially involve thousands of people traveling over long distances at the public expense, and Constantius could easily call two of them in a year. Remember Sozomen's description of the incalculable number of priests and deacons and others who showed up at Nicaea, and you can begin to imagine the effect all these synods had on the functions of government. No wonder Ammianus was annoyed. He probably had to fly coach.

Eusebius of Nicomedia Plots

Constantius was the emperor whom Athanasius would have to deal with for the next twenty-four years.

It was obvious from the beginning of his reign that things would not go smoothly for the Catholic side. Constantius had been out of town when Alexander died and Paul became bishop of Constantinople. When he returned, the Arians had all sorts of bad things to say about Paul. And Constantius listened to them. A local council was called — Constantius's first council — and Paul was deposed. In his place, the new bishop of Constantinople was Eusebius of Nicomedia.

Athanasius, meanwhile, had come back to Alexandria. But he wouldn't get much peace. "Those who were attached to the Arian doctrines were thrown into consternation and could not keep the peace; they excited continuous seditions, and had recourse to other machinations against him. The partisans of Eusebius accused him before the emperor of being a seditious person, and of having reversed the decree of exile, contrary to the laws of the church, and without the consent of the bishops."[4]

The Arians also sent ambassadors to Pope Julius in Rome, hoping to get him to denounce Athanasius. Another group came from Egypt in favor of Athanasius and made their case before Pope Julius. He responded by inviting the Eastern bishops to a synod in Rome to discuss the Athanasius question. (They decided not to come.)

The Council of Antioch

Meanwhile, Eusebius kept constant pressure on the emperor Constantius: Athanasius had to go. In 341, another council was held at Antioch, where Constantius had just finished a magnificent church:

> Constantine began to build it during his lifetime, and as the structure had been just finished by his son Constantius, it was deemed a favorable opportunity by the partisans of Eusebius [of Nicomedia], who had been eager for it for a long time, to convene a council. They therefore met together in Antioch, with those from various regions who held their opinions; their bishops were about ninety-seven in number. Their professed object was the consecration of the newly finished church; but they intended nothing else than the abolition of the decrees of the Nicene Council, and this was fully proved by what followed.[5]

Constantius himself presided. Here the Eusebian party began to unveil their new strategy. They were perfect Nicene Christians, they said. And they weren't followers of Arius. He was just a priest; they were bishops. How could they be followers of that nobody Arius? So what they believed was compatible with the Nicene definition of the Faith, and you could take their word for it.

> They resorted, in fact, to such ambiguity of expression that neither the Arians nor the followers of the decrees of the Nicene Council could call the arrangement of their words into question, as though they were ignorant of the holy Scriptures. They purposely avoided all forms of expression which were rejected by either party, and only made use of those which were universally admitted. They confessed that the Son is with the Father, that He is the only begotten One, and that He is God, and existed before all things; and that He took flesh upon Him, and fulfilled the will of His Father. They confessed these and similar truths, but they did not describe the doctrine of the Son being co-eternal or consubstantial with the Father, or the opposite.[6]

This was the new tactic of the Eusebian party: State that you agree with the Nicene Council, but don't actually repeat the parts of its definitions that offended Arians the most.

Then the bishops proceeded to the main business, which was getting rid of Athanasius. They settled on someone named Gregory of Cappadocia to replace him as bishop of Alexandria. He was sent off to Alexandria "with a large body of soldiers"[7] supposedly to keep him safe, but probably at least as much to crush all possible opposition.

Athanasius himself describes what happened when the news reached Alexandria:

> While we were holding our assemblies in peace, as usual, and while the people were rejoicing in them, and advancing in godly conversation, and while our fellow-ministers in Egypt, and the Thebaid, and Libya, were in love and peace both with one another and with us — all of a sudden the Prefect of Egypt puts out a public letter, bearing the form of an edict, and declaring that one Gregory from Cappadocia was coming to be my successor from the court. This announcement confounded everyone, for such

a proceeding was entirely novel, and now heard of for the first time.

The people, however, assembled still more constantly in the churches, for they very well knew that neither they themselves, nor any bishop or priest, nor in short anyone had ever complained against me; and they saw that Arians only were on his side, and were aware also that he was himself an Arian, and was sent by Eusebius and his fellows to the Arian party. For you know, brethren, that Eusebius and his fellows have always been the supporters and associates of the impious heresy of the Arian madmen, by whose means they have always carried on their designs against me, and were the authors of my banishment into Gaul.[8]

Bloody riots followed. Athanasius tells us that the imperial officials seized all the church property by violence, and the various mobs in Alexandria, always ready to erupt, took advantage of the disorder:

The church and the holy baptistery were set on fire, and straightway groans, shrieks, and lamentations, were heard through the city; while the citizens in their indignation at these enormities, cried shame upon the governor, and protested against the violence used to them. For holy and undefiled virgins were being stripped naked, and suffering treatment which is not to be named, and if they resisted, they were in danger of their lives. Monks were being trampled under foot and perishing; some were being hurled headlong; others were being destroyed with swords and clubs; others were being wounded and beaten. … Certain impious men also, following the examples set them in the bitterest persecutions, were seizing upon the virgins and ascetics by the hands and dragging them along, and as they were hauling them, tried to make them blaspheme and deny the Lord; and when they refused to do so, were beating them violently and trampling them under foot.

Then they came looking for Athanasius. But Athanasius, stubborn as he could be, was not fool enough to sit down and wait to be slaughtered.

When all this was done, they did not stop even here, but conferred about how they might do the same thing in the other church where I was mostly living during those days. And they were eager to extend their fury to this church as well, so that they might hunt out and dispatch me. And this would have been my fate, had not the grace of Christ assisted me, if it were only that I might escape to relate these few particulars concerning their conduct.

For seeing that they were exceedingly mad against me, and being anxious that the church should not be injured, nor the virgins that were in it suffer, nor additional murders be committed, nor the people again outraged, I withdrew myself from among them, remembering the words of our Savior, "When they persecute you in one town, flee to the next" (Mt 10:23). For I knew, from the evil they had done against the first-named church, that they would forbear no outrage against the other also.

And there in fact they reverenced not even the Lord's day of the holy Feast [Easter], but in that church also they imprisoned the persons who belonged to it, at a time when the Lord delivered all from the bonds of death, whereas Gregory and his associates, as if fighting against our Savior, and depending upon the patronage of the Governor, have turned into mourning this day of liberty to the servants of Christ. The heathens were rejoicing to do this, for they abhor that day; and perhaps Gregory was only carrying out the commands of Eusebius and his fellows in forcing the Christians to mourn under the infliction of bonds.

With these acts of violence has the Governor seized upon the churches, and has given them up to Gregory and the Arian madmen.[9]

Athanasius managed to make it out of the city alive and head for Rome, where he hoped for some protection from Pope Julius and Constans, Constantius's brother, who had been friendly to him before.

This would be Exile Number Two.

5.

Support from the West

By now, the Eusebians had bishops in the three most important sees in the East: Alexandria, Antioch, and Constantinople. Historians sometimes call the Eusebians Semi-Arians because they backed off on some of Arius's most extreme assertions and claimed to be the reasonable centrist party, as opposed to that fanatic Athanasius.

But they were never a popular party. The fact that Gregory of Cappadocia had to be imposed on Alexandria by violence shows what the ordinary Christians of the time thought of the reasonable centrists.

Meanwhile, Athanasius was welcomed in Rome. The machinations in the East did not sit well with the Western Church:

> The ruler of the Church at Rome and all the priests of the West regarded these deeds as a personal insult; for they had accorded from the beginning with all the decisions in the vote made by those convened at Nicaea, nor did they now cease from that way of thinking. On the arrival of Athanasius, they received him kindly, and took up his cause among themselves.[1]

Pope Julius wrote to Eusebius of Nicomedia defending Athanasius. Eusebius and his circle responded with a letter more or less daring him to call a council and judge Athanasius for himself. But the letter was written in such arrogant terms that everyone at Rome who read it was shocked. "I have read your letter," Julius wrote back, "which was brought to me by my priests Elpidius and Philoxenus, and I am surprised to find that, whereas I wrote to you in charity and with conscious sincerity, you have replied to me in an unbecoming and contentious temper; for the pride and arrogance of the writers is plainly exhibited in that letter. … Your attitude forces us to conclude that, even in the terms in which you appeared to pay honor to us, you were being sarcastic."

The letter was quite long and detailed and summarized all the injustices that had been committed against Athanasius in particular and the Eastern Church in general. "Bishops are forced away from their sees and driven into banishment, while others from different quarters are appointed in their place; others are treacherously assailed, so that the people have to grieve for those who are forcibly taken from them, while, as to those who are sent in their room, they are obliged to give over seeking the man whom they desire, and to receive those they do not."[2]

Eusebius of Nicomedia never read the letter. By the time it reached Constantinople, Eusebius was dead.

Tumult in Constantinople

As soon as the news broke in Constantinople that Eusebius had died, a mob gathered and brought the exiled bishop Paul back to the cathedral in triumph. But an Arian mob also gathered.

> At the same time those of the opposing multitude seized this occasion and came together in another church, among whom were the adherents of

Theognis, bishop of Nicaea, of Theodore, bishop
of Heraclea, and others of the same party who
chanced to be present, and they ordained Macedonius bishop of Constantinople. This excited frequent seditions in the city which assumed all the
appearance of a war, for the people fell upon one
another, and many perished. The city was filled
with tumult, so that the emperor, who was then
at Antioch, on hearing of what had occurred, was
moved to wrath, and issued a decree for the expul-
sion of Paul. Hermogenes, general of the cavalry,
endeavored to put this edict of the emperor's into
execution; for having been sent to Thrace, he had,
on the journey, to pass by Constantinople, and he
thought, by means of his army, to eject Paul from
the church by force. But the people, instead of
yielding, met him with open resistance, and while
the soldiers, in order to carry out the orders they
had received, attempted still greater violence, the
insurgents entered the house of Hermogenes, set
fire to it, killed him, and tying a rope to his body,
dragged it through the city.[3]

Constantius, who had been in Antioch, was furious, of
course. He was furious at Paul and had him thrown out

of the city. But he was also furious at Macedonius for allowing himself to be ordained without the emperor's approval.

Athanasius Introduces Monasticism

Meanwhile, while he was in the West, Athanasius was not idle. In fact, he was changing the history of the world, although nobody would have recognized it at the time. As he met with various bishops and other Christians, he told stories about the heroic monks in Egypt — heroes such as his old friend Saint Anthony. The Westerners were enthralled. The idea caught their imagination, and the fire of Western monasticism was ignited. Decades later, Saint Jerome wrote a eulogy for his friend Marcella, who had set up a Christian community in Rome, and noted that she had gotten the idea from Athanasius and his retinue of Alexandrian refugees:

> None of the noble ladies at Rome knew anything about the monastic life, or had dared to take it up, because of the ignominious novelty of the thing, as it was thought in those days: the very name of it was vile among the people. From some Alexandrian priests and Athanasius, and later from Peter, who had fled from the per-

secution of the Arian heretics to Rome, which seemed to be the safest place for their communion, she learned of the life of the blessed Anthony (then still living), and the monasteries of Pachomius in the Thebaid and the discipline of the virgins and widows there.[4]

Of course, the monasteries in the West would go on to be the last refuges of civilization and culture when the Roman Empire fell apart. When we hear the story of Athanasius standing almost alone against the onslaught of Arianism, we shouldn't forget that he found time to accomplish other things as well.

Athanasius was treated as a visiting celebrity in the West, and the bishops there did take up his cause as if it were their own. In 343, a council at Sardica (today's Sofia, the capital of Bulgaria) examined his case, but Athanasius's accusers walked out. They formed a countercouncil in the suburbs and declared the term *homoousios* anathema. The main council at Sardica declared Athanasius reinstated; the Eastern bishops blew a raspberry in its direction.

But by this time, more than bishops were involved. In our time, the case of Athanasius would be a religious dispute. But there was no division between religion and politics in his time, as we've seen, and the Emperor of the West was starting to take an interest in the case.

Constans and Constantius were always uneasy part-ners at best. Constantius had leaned heavily on the Arian side; Constans was staunchly on the side of the ortho-dox Catholic Church. Doubtless the bishops who saw him frequently took every opportunity to mention the injustices that had been perpetrated against Athanasius, and they worked him up into righteous indignation.

In 344, Constans wrote to his brother to demand that Athanasius — and Paul, the exiled bishop of Con-stantinople, as well — be reinstated. He did not beat around the bush. "Don't make me come over there," he told his big brother:

> Athanasius and Paul are here with me; and I am quite satisfied after investigation, that they are persecuted for the sake of piety. If, there-fore, you will pledge yourself to reinstate them in their sees, and to punish those who have so unjustly injured them, I will send them to you; but should you refuse to do this, be assured that I will myself come over there and restore them to their own sees, in spite of your opposition.[5]

Had Athanasius himself put him up to it? Well, Athanasius had met with Constans. But, years later, justifying his conduct to Constantius, Athanasius would insist that it had been Constans's idea:

> When I left Alexandria, I did not go to your brother's headquarters, or to any other persons, but only to Rome; and having laid my case before the Church (for this was my only concern), I spent my time in the public worship. I did not write to your brother, except when Eusebius and his fellows had written to him to accuse me, and I was compelled while yet at Alexandria to defend myself; and again when I sent to him volumes containing the holy Scriptures, which he had ordered me to prepare for him. It behooves me, while I defend my conduct, to tell the truth to your Piety. When, however, three years had passed away, he wrote to me in the fourth year, commanding me to meet him (he was then at Milan); and when I asked the reason (for I was ignorant of it, the Lord is my witness), I learned that certain bishops had gone up and requested him to write to your Piety desiring that a Council might be called. Believe me, Sire, this is the

truth of the matter; I am not lying. Accordingly, I went down to Milan, and met with great kindness from him; for he condescended to see me, and to say that he had dispatched letters to you, requesting that a Council might be called. And while I remained in that city, he sent for me again into Gaul (for the father Hosius was going that way), that we might travel from there to Sardica. And after the Council, he wrote to me while I stayed at Naissus, and I went up, and lived afterwards at Aquileia; where the letters of your Piety found me. And again, being invited from there by your departed brother, I returned into Gaul, and so came at length to your Piety.[6]

Whether Athanasius had asked for it or not, the letter from Constans put Constantius in an awkward position. He had enough troubles right now without getting into a fight with the Emperor of the West. Later on, Athanasius would be accused of having slandered Constantius to Constans, but he denied this vigorously:

I have never spoken evil of your Piety before your brother Constans, the most religious Augustus of blessed memory. I did not exasperate

him against you, as these have falsely accused
me. But whenever in my interviews with him he
has mentioned your Grace (and he did mention
you at the time that Thalassus came to Patavia,
and I was staying at Aquileia), the Lord is witness, how I spoke of your Piety in terms which
I would that God would reveal unto your soul,
that you might condemn the falsehood of these
my calumniators. Bear with me, most gracious
Augustus, and freely grant me your indulgence
while I speak of this matter. Your most Christian brother was not a man of so light a temper, nor was I a person of such a character, that
we should communicate together on a subject
like this, or that I should slander a brother to a
brother, or speak evil of an emperor before an
emperor.[7]

Athanasius's defense shows us how difficult it was to
navigate the relationships between Constantine's sons.
On the one hand, they had all wanted to kill each other.
On the other hand, Constantius would not tolerate anyone else's suggesting that all was not peace and harmony
between them.

Constantius's awkward situation was relieved a little

when, in 345, the very unpopular Gregory of Cappadocia died. Some sources suggest he was murdered. That left the see of Alexandria unambiguously open for Athanasius's return without displacing anybody. Constantius gave in and wrote Athanasius a nice letter asking him to come back and lead the Church in Alexandria:

> Constantius Victor Augustus to Athanasius the bishop.
>
> Our compassionate clemency cannot permit you to be any longer tossed and disquieted as it were by the boisterous waves of the sea. Our unwearied piety has not been unmindful of you driven from your native home, despoiled of your property, and wandering in pathless solitudes. And although I have too long deferred acquainting you by letter with the purpose of my mind, expecting your coming to us of your own accord to seek a remedy for your troubles; yet since fear perhaps has hindered you from carrying out your wishes, we therefore have sent to your reverence letters full of indulgence, in order that you may fearlessly hasten to appear in our presence, whereby after experiencing our benevolence, you may attain your desire, and be

reestablished in your proper position. For this reason I have requested my Lord and brother Constans Victor Augustus to grant you permission to come, to the end that by the consent of us both you may be restored to your country, having this assurance of our favor.[8]

To smooth the way home, Constantius also wrote letters to the Alexandrians, specifying that all the decrees against Athanasius and his friends were annulled:

Constantius, Victor, Maximus, Augustus, to the Bishops and Priests of the Catholic Church.

The most reverend Athanasius has not been deserted by the grace of God, but although for a brief season he was subjected to trial to which human nature is liable, he has obtained from the all-surveying Providence such an answer to his prayers as was meet, and is restored by the will of the Most High, and by our sentence, both to his country and to the church over which by divine permission he presided. Wherefore, in accordance with this, it is fitting that it should be provided by our clemency, that all the decrees which have heretofore been passed against those who held communion with him, be now consigned to oblivion, and that all suspicions respecting them be henceforward set at rest, and that immunity, such as the Clergy who are associated with him formerly enjoyed, be duly confirmed to them. Moreover to our other acts of favor towards him we have thought good to add the following, that all persons of the sacred catalogue should understand, that an assurance of safety is given to all who adhere to him, whether bishops, or other clergy. And union with him will be a sufficient guarantee, in the case of any person, of an upright intention. For whoever, acting according to a better judgment and part, shall choose to hold communion with him, we order, in imitation of that Providence which has already gone before, that all such should have the advantage of the grace which by the will of the Most High is now offered to them from us. May God preserve you.

Back in Alexandria

Athanasius reached Alexandria in 346 and was welcomed back by cheering fans. His homecoming was a parade and a holiday and a giant party.

For a couple of years after Athanasius's return, things were peaceful in Alexandria — at least as peaceful as things ever were in that city. But the enemies of Athanasius were not going to give up.

They were encouraged in the year 350 when a disaster happened in the West. A rebel emperor, Magnentius, seized the throne and killed Constans (probably sparing Constantius the trouble). He then went on a rampage in Rome and killed everyone he suspected of plotting against him. To be fair to him, a lot of prominent Romans were conspiring against him, since by all accounts he was an awful tyrant.

Later, Athanasius would be accused of corresponding with the usurper Magnentius. This charge, if we take Athanasius at his word, blindsided him. The charge moved him to a characteristic fit of sarcasm, reminding us that one of the traits the people who knew him always mentioned about Athanasius was his quick sense of humor:

> But for the traitor Magnentius, the Lord is witness, and his Anointed is witness, I do not know him, nor was I ever acquainted with him. So how could there be any correspondence between two people so entirely unacquainted with each

other? What reason was there for me to write to a man like that? How could I have begun my letter if I *had* written to him? What could I have said? "That was a good thing you did, murdering the man who honored me, whose kindness I shall never forget"? Or, "I approve of your conduct in destroying our Christian friends, and most faithful brethren"? Or, "I really liked the way you butchered the people who so kindly entertained me at Rome"?[9]

Not long after Constans died, Pope Julius died as well. That deprived Athanasius of his two most powerful friends in the West. While Constans was alive, his threat to force Athanasius down Constantius's throat if he had to would have to be in the background in Constantius's thinking. Now that there was open war between East and West anyway (since Constantius was not willing to accept the murderer of his brother as his co-emperor), that variable was removed from his calculations. As for Pope Julius, he had been rock-solid in his support of Athanasius, and the pope in Rome mattered in a way that no other single bishop did. Julius was replaced by Liberius, who was also an orthodox Catholic — but perhaps not rock-solid.

Constantius defeated Magnentius in 353, becoming sole emperor of the Roman world. The Arian bishops saw their opportunity to step up their campaign. Soon Constantius was wholly under the influence of the Arians again.

The first big victim was not Athanasius but Paul, the aged bishop of Constantinople, whom Constans had also insisted on restoring. An imperial prefect summoned him and, with no preparation, packed him into a boat and sent him out of the city. The next morning, soldiers hacked their way through the mob to reinstall Macedonius as bishop over a pile of dead bodies. Paul was sent far away and never heard from again. The word was that he had been strangled. Supporters of Macedonius claimed that Paul had died naturally of the hardships of exile, which really isn't all that much better.

Constantius, meanwhile, having defeated his last rival, had time to indulge in his favorite hobby of sponsoring synods and councils. But he lost patience with the debate part of the procedure. He began to claim that he himself had the divinely inspired truth. He expected the bishops to gather to give him a ceremonial confirmation of his already-formed opinion. They could debate as much as they liked, but if they took the wrong side, they would be banished or tortured until they understood why they were wrong.

He brought together a council at Milan, for example, to condemn Athanasius. As we already saw, he was
charged with slandering Constantius to his late lament-
ed brother and with treasonably corresponding with the
usurper Magnentius. If those charges wouldn't stick, he
was charged with having celebrated Mass in a church
that had not yet been dedicated, which was somehow
construed as blasphemy and an insult to the emperor
himself. And the old slanders of dabbling in black magic
seem to have been not far in the background:

> The Eastern bishops insisted that Athanasius
> should be condemned to banishment, and ex-
> pelled from Alexandria; and the others, either
> from fear, fraud, or ignorance, assented to the
> measure. Dionysius, bishop of Alba, the metropo-
> lis of Italy, Eusebius, bishop of Vercella in Liguria,
> Paulinus, bishop of Treves, Rhodanus, and Luci-
> fer, were the only bishops who protested against
> this decision; and they declared that Athanasius
> ought not to be condemned on such slight pre-
> texts; and that the evil would not cease with his
> condemnation; but that those who supported
> the orthodox doctrines concerning the Godhead

would be forthwith subjected to a plot. They represented that the whole measure was a scheme concerted by the emperor and the Arians with the view of suppressing the Nicene faith. Their boldness was punished by an edict of immediate banishment, and Hilary was exiled with them. The result too plainly showed for what purpose the council of Milan had been convened. For the councils which were held shortly after at Ariminum and Seleucia were evidently designed to change the doctrines established by the Nicene council, as I shall directly show.[10]

By now, Constantius had become almost insanely obsessed with Athanasius. His treatment of Pope Liberius shows us just how obsessed he was and how intent on having his own way. We'll hear it first from our old friend Ammianus Marcellinus, the pagan historian.

Ammianus obviously had no opinions on the Christian dispute over the Trinity. He figured that Athanasius must be some sort of troublemaker, since trouble followed him wherever he went, and he gives us a good sense of what the reputation of Athanasius was at the imperial court. But even Ammianus found it hard to stomach the way Constantius treated the pope.

Liberius, a priest of the Christian law, was ordered by Constantius to be brought before the council, as one who had resisted the commands of the emperor, and the decrees of many of his own colleagues, in an affair which I will explain briefly.

Athanasius was at that time bishop of Alexandria; and as he was a man who sought to magnify himself above his profession, and to mix himself up with affairs which did not belong to his province, as continual reports made known, an assembly of many of his sect met together — a synod, as they call it — and deprived him of the right of administering the sacraments, which he previously enjoyed.

For it was said that he, being very deeply skilled in the arts of prophecy and the interpretation of auguries and omens, had very often predicted coming events. And to these charges were added others very inconsistent with the laws of the religion over which he presided.

So Liberius, being of the same opinion with those who condemned these practices, was ordered, by the sentence of the emperor, to expel Athanasius from his priestly seat; but this he

firmly refused to do, reiterating the assertion
that it was the extremity of wickedness to condemn a man who had neither been brought before any court nor been heard in his defence,
in this openly resisting the commands of the
emperor.

For that prince, being always unfavourable
to Athanasius, although he knew that what he
ordered had in fact taken effect, yet was exceedingly desirous that it should be confirmed by
that authority which the bishops of the Eternal
City enjoy, as being of higher rank. And as he
did not succeed in this, Liberius was removed by
night; a measure which was not accomplished
without great difficulty, through the fear which
his enemies had of the people, among whom he
was exceedingly popular.[11]

Athanasius, of course, heard about all these movements
against him. By this point, he was not willing to trust
his safety to the mercy of Constantius, so there was no
question of going to the emperor personally to ask for
justice. But he sent a delegation of other Egyptian bishops, including his old friend Serapion, to speak to Constantius.

They had hardly left when letters from the emperor came in, demanding that Athanasius present himself at the imperial palace. "Athanasius and all the people of the Church were greatly troubled at this command," says Sozomen, "for they considered that no safety could be enjoyed when acting either in obedience or in disobedience to an emperor of heterodox sentiments." However, it was "determined that he should remain at Alexandria, and the bearer of the letters left the city without having effected anything."[12]

In a few months, Constantius took more forceful measures. He sent a messenger to demand that Athanasius leave Alexandria. When the messenger returned with news that the people of Alexandria would riot if Athanasius was removed, Constantius sent an army.

Things had come to the point where the Roman emperor felt he had to send an army to get rid of one bishop.

The army was under the command of a general named Syrianus, and he was accompanied by the imperial notary Hilary. When they demanded that Athanasius leave, he made a very sensible demand in return: Show me the emperor's orders.

The emperor had not sent any written orders. He figured an army would convey his message clearly enough.

But Athanasius had the letters Constantius had sent him a few years back, telling him that it was the emperor's wish that he should remain bishop of Alexandria. Those were *his* orders, he said. The mob in Alexandria loudly backed him: Show us the emperor's orders.

In a letter he later wrote to Constantius, Athanasius himself tells us how it went from there:

> When they persisted in their demand, Syrianus at last perceived the reasonableness of it, and consented, protesting by your safety (Hilary was present and witnessed this) that he would put an end to the disturbance, and refer the case to your Piety. …
>
> All demanded that the letters of your Piety should be exhibited. For although the bare word of an emperor is of equal weight and authority with his written command, especially if he who reports it, boldly affirms in writing that it has been given him; yet when they neither openly declared that they had received any command, nor, as they were requested to do, gave me assurance of it in writing, but acted altogether as by their own authority; I confess, I say it boldly, I was suspicious of them. For there were many

Arians about them, who were their companions at table, and their counselors; and while they attempted nothing openly, they were preparing to assail me by stratagem and treachery. Nor did they act at all as under the authority of a royal command, but, as their conduct betrayed, at the solicitation of enemies. This made me demand more urgently that they should produce letters from you, seeing that all their undertakings and designs were of a suspicious nature; and because it was unseemly that after I had entered the Church, under the authority of so many letters from you, I should retire from it without such a sanction. When however Syrianus gave his promise, all the people assembled together in the Churches with feelings of joyfulness and security.

But twenty-three days after, he burst into the Church with his soldiers, while we were engaged in our usual services, as those who entered in there witnessed; for it was a vigil, preparatory to a communion on the morrow. And such things were done that night as the Arians desired and had beforehand denounced against us. For the General brought them with him; and they were the instigators and advisers of the attack. This is no incredible story of mine, most religious Augustus; for it was not done in secret, but was noised abroad everywhere. When therefore I saw the assault begun, I first exhorted the people to retire, and then withdrew myself after them, God hiding and guiding me, as those who were with me at the time witness. Since then, I have remained by myself, though I have all confidence to answer for my conduct, in the first place before God, and also before your Piety, for that I did not flee and desert my people, but can point to the attack of the General upon us, as a proof of persecution. His proceedings have caused the greatest astonishment among all men; for either he ought not to have made a promise, or not to have broken it after he had made it.[13]

There were people who blamed Athanasius for running away. To those people, Athanasius had a short and sensible answer: "Let them stop trying to kill me, and I'll stop running away."

Athanasius went into hiding. Another Cappadocian, this time George of Cappadocia, was sent to replace him.

This would be Exile Number Three.

6.
Interesting Times

George of Cappadocia proved to be a tyrant who made almost everyone in Alexandria hate him. He was zealously antipagan, so the pagan mob hated him. The Jewish mob hated him. The Catholic mob hated him. He seemed to have thought that he had been made king of Alexandria, not just bishop of the Christian Church there.

"He ruled by force rather than by priestly moderation," says Sozomen; "and as he strove to strike terror into the minds of the people, and carried on a cruel persecution against the followers of Athanasius, and, moreover, imprisoned and maimed many men and women, he was accounted a tyrant."[1] Naturally, riots resulted; Athanasius's supporters took over the churches, and George ran away; Constantius sent an army to put George back in place. After that, George seems to have hated the people of Alexandria as much as they hated him, and there was no limit to his sadistic whims and his insatiable greed.

In his exile, Athanasius was still productive. In fact, the orthodox Catholic side seems to have recognized him as an authority on what it meant to be really orthodox and really Christian. It was probably during this exile that he wrote his letters to Serapion on the divinity of the Holy Spirit. The controversy about the divinity of Christ was vexing enough, but now bishops were having to deal with people who denied that the Spirit was part of the divine Trinity. According to Sozomen, the Arians took the wrong side, whether they were the Arian extremists or the milder ones who were content to say that the Son is *like* the Father:

> Many contentions and debates ensued on this subject, similar to those which had been held concerning the nature of God the Word. Those

who asserted that the Son is *dissimilar* from the Father, and those who insisted that He is *similar* in substance to the Father, came to one common opinion concerning the Holy Ghost; for both parties maintained that the Holy Ghost differs in substance, and that He is but the Minister and the third in point of order, honor, and substance. Those, on the contrary, who believed that the Son is *consubstantial* with the Father also held the same view about the Spirit.[2]

Athanasius applied his usual reasoning skills — and his usual vigorous rhetoric — to explain to Serapion exactly where those people were wrong.

Meanwhile, interesting times were on the way. To understand them, though, we'll have to dredge up some backstory.

The Unusual Childhood of Julian

When he became emperor at the age of twenty, as we remember, Constantius had taken care to kill all his near relations and anyone else he thought might try to claim the throne. The only ones he spared were two boys too young to be a threat. One of them was his cousin Julian, an orphan since Constantius had murdered his father.

Julian lived a sheltered life for much of his childhood. He was kept far away from the center of government and closely watched, though his cage was certainly gilded. His guardian early on was Eusebius of Nicomedia.

Constantius didn't mind Julian's getting a good education. As long as he had his nose in a book, he wasn't a threat to Constantius. A neighbor, George of Cappadocia, allowed him the use of his extensive library of standard Greek literature. George would later pay a high price for his kindness.

When Julian was in his middle twenties, Constantius appointed him caesar, a sort of deputy emperor, and sent him to fight the Germans in Gaul. Actually, Constantius had no intention of giving Julian any real power. He left plenty of minions to surround Julian and keep him in line.

But Julian turned out to be a natural commander, and he led his army to repeated victories. Not surprisingly, they decided he would make a better emperor than the far-off Constantius, who, though he had won battles with Roman opponents, mostly lost battles with barbarians. In 360, they proclaimed Julian Augustus, meaning that a civil war with Constantius was inevitable.

Then a kind of miracle occurred. While he was leading his army eastward to face Constantius, Julian heard that Constantius had died of natural causes — and that he had left the empire to Julian. Suddenly, without a battle, he was sole emperor of the Roman world.

Julian Turns the Clock Back

All this would be just another of the many messy imperial successions in history, except that Julian's peculiar education had left him with some peculiar ideas. To the amazement of the whole Roman world, and the horror of the Christians, Julian announced that he had become a "Hellene" — a follower of the ancient Greek gods.

When the news reached Alexandria, the pagan mob was jubilant. In the celebrations that followed, they jubilantly slaughtered George of Cappadocia, the Arian bishop who had replaced Athanasius and the man whose extensive library had made Julian acquainted with the tales of the old gods.* The mob trampled and kicked and tore George to pieces, along with two imperial officials. George had certainly been obnoxious to the pagans, pillaging their temples and stopping their celebrations. But he was also the most visible Christian, and it's quite possible that Athanasius would have suffered the same fate if he had been there at the time. On the other hand, as our pagan friend Ammianus Marcellinus points out,

*This is assuming that it was the same George.

"In truth the wretched men who underwent such cruel punishment might have been protected by the aid of the Christians, if both parties had not been equally exasperated by hatred of George."[3]

Meanwhile, Julian lost no time in turning the Roman Empire upside down. He ordered the pagan temples restored and reopened. He tried to set up a kind of pagan church on the model of the Christian Church, but with more gods. To keep the Christians occupied, he canceled all the exiles and allowed all the Christian leaders — Catholic or Arian or whatever — to come back to their homes. According to our old friend Ammianus Marcellinus (who, in spite of his religious sympathies, wasn't a big fan of Julian), the motive was more than just liberality and fairness:

> And to increase the effect of his arrangements, he ordered the priests of the different Christian sects, with the adherents of each sect, to be admitted into the palace, and rather politely expressed his wish that, their dissensions being appeased, each without any hindrance might fearlessly follow the religion he preferred. He did this the more resolutely because, as long license increased their dissensions, he thought

> he should never have to fear the unanimity of
> the common people, having found by experi-
> ence that no wild beasts are so hostile to men
> as Christian sects in general are to one another.[4]

Since the exiles were allowed to come back, Athanasius
figured that applied to him. He returned to Alexandria
and was welcomed by a huge crowd of enthusiastic
Christians.

When Julian heard it, he hit the roof. Julian hated
Athanasius at least as much as the Arians did, and possibly more.

Julian Hates Athanasius Too

Why? What made Athanasius, out of all the Christians,
such an enemy to the man who professed to find the
"Galileans" — his insulting name for Christians — be-
neath his contempt? Whatever it was, when he found out
that Athanasius had come back to Alexandria as bishop,
Julian wrote an edict in the form of a rather snippy letter
to the people of Alexandria:

> One who had been banished by so many impe-
> rial decrees issued by many Emperors ought to
> have waited for at least one imperial edict, and

then on the strength of that returned to his own country, and not displayed rashness and folly, and insulted the laws as though they did not exist. For we have not, even now, granted to the Galileans who were exiled by Constantius of blessed memory to return to their churches, but only to their own countries. Yet I learn that the most audacious Athanasius, puffed up with his usual insolence, has again seized what is called among them the episcopal throne, and that this is not a little displeasing to the god-fearing citizens [meaning the pagan citizens] of Alexandria. Wherefore we publicly warn him to depart from the city immediately, on the very day that he shall receive this letter of our clemency. But if he remains within the city, we publicly warn him that he will receive a much greater and more severe punishment.[5]

Athanasius did not leave right away, and Julian (known now as Julian the Apostate) was very annoyed. He wrote a letter to Ecdicius, the prefect of Egypt, telling him to take care of this Athanasius problem — and from it we may get a hint about why Julian really hated Athanasius so much. Many centuries later, we remember Athanasius for his long battles with Arianism. But he was also very effective in the main business of a Christian teacher, which was making more Christians. He was converting "Hellenes" to Christianity even during the Apostate's reign. It made Julian boil with rage, as we can tell from the note he scribbled at the end of his official orders:

> Even though you do not write to me on other matters, you ought at least to have written about that enemy of the gods, Athanasius, especially since, for a long time past, you have known my just decrees. I swear by mighty Serapis that, if Athanasius the enemy of the gods does not depart from that city, or rather from all Egypt, before the December Kalends, I shall fine the cohort which you command a hundred pounds of gold. And you know that, though I am slow to condemn, I am even much slower to remit when I have once condemned. *Added with his own hand.* It really irks me that my orders are neglected. By all the gods, there's nothing I'd be so glad to see you do — or I mean I'd like to hear you'd already done it — as expelling Athanasius beyond the frontiers of Egypt. That filthy brute! He's had the audacity to baptize Hellene women

of rank during my reign! Throw him out![6]

(Here the Christian who copied the manuscript centuries later could not contain himself any longer, and he scribbled his own angry apostrophe to Julian: "This is a saint, you filthy dog and three-times cursed apostate and three times miserable man!")

Julian's orders were quite clear. But the Catholic Christians of Alexandria had been delighted to have their bishop back, and they decided they would send a petition to the emperor begging him to let Athanasius come back again. After all, Julian loved to tell everybody what a mild and reasonable emperor he was. Perhaps he would listen to the polite request of his citizens.

The reply they got showed them the real Julian. He began by scolding them for being Christians at all. Their city was founded by the great Alexander, and the gods had been worshiped there for centuries. "I am overwhelmed with shame, I affirm it by the gods, O men of Alexandria, to think that even a single Alexandrian can admit that he is a Galilean." He gave them a long and pedantic lecture about the benefits the pagan gods had given their city, and what had Christianity ever done for them? He reminded them that he had been a Christian himself but got over it. "For you will not stray from the right road if you listen to someone who till his twentieth year walked in that road of yours, but for twelve years now has walked in this road I speak of, by the grace of the gods."

Then, finally, he came to the point: You can have anybody but Athanasius.

Therefore, if it pleases you to obey me, you will rejoice me the more. But if you choose to persevere in the superstition and instruction of wicked men, at least agree among yourselves not to crave for Athanasius. In any case there are many of his pupils who can comfort well enough those itching ears of yours that yearn to hear impious words. I only wish that, along with Athanasius, the wickedness of his impious school had been suppressed. But as it is you have a fine crowd of them and need have no trouble. For any man you pick out of the crowd will be in no way inferior to him for whom you crave, at any rate for the teaching of the scriptures. But if you have made these requests because you are so fond of the general subtlety of Athanasius — for I am informed that the man is a clever rascal — then you must know that this is exactly why he has been banished from the city. A meddle-some man is unfit by nature to be leader of the people. But if this leader is not even a man but only a contemptible puppet, like this great personage who thinks he is risking his head, this surely gives the signal for disorder. Wherefore, that nothing of the sort may occur in your case, as I long ago gave orders that he depart from the city, I now say, let him depart from the whole of Egypt.

Let this be publicly proclaimed to my citizens of Alexandria.[7]

So Athanasius slipped away again. "This is just a little cloud that will pass away," Athanasius told his friends.

It was a pretty big cloud while it lasted, though. Julian wasn't going to let Athanasius just slip away. He had his imperial storm troopers running all over Egypt looking for the runaway bishop.

So Athanasius was in hiding again. This would be Exile Number Four.

7.
A Brief Triumph

There's a story about Athanasius's flight that may or may not be true, but it certainly seems characteristic. The story goes like this: Athanasius was going up the Nile away from his pursuers, and he heard that they had nearly caught up with him. His friends told him to land and run into the desert, but Athanasius told them to turn the boat around.

It sounded crazy, but they did it.

Soon the boat full of soldiers came up the river.

"Have you seen Athanasius?" one of the soldiers

shouted from the boat

"You're very close to him," Athanasius shouted back. "Keep going, and you'll catch him."

And so, without lying directly, Athanasius slipped right past the search party and went on his way.[1]

The imperial investigators searched all over Egypt for Athanasius, but he was safely hidden among his old friends the monks in the desert. Meanwhile, Julian was making life worse and worse for Christians — and for many other people, since he was planning to conquer Persia and needed to collect quite a bit in taxes to finance his expedition.

The Persian Expedition

Rome and Persia had been almost constantly at war for hundreds of years. Julian, though, had grown up reading the adventures of Alexander the Great, and he decided that he would be able to repeat Alexander's feat of subjugating the whole Persian Empire.

His expedition started well. He moved as fast as his soldiers could march, so he was in Persia before the Persians even knew what hit them. Once he was there, he won a string of victories while marching farther and farther into Persia.

Speed and distance ultimately bogged him down.

The Persians destroyed all the crops and supplies in the country he was marching through, and he had come too far to be resupplied easily from home. His expedition was already in pretty bad shape when Julian was killed in battle.

When that happened, the air went out of the Roman army. They chose a soldier named Jovian to replace Julian as emperor. He took a look at the situation and realized there was no good way out of it. So he agreed to a humiliating peace with Persia that shrank the Roman Empire in exchange for getting his army out alive.

Jovian's New Deal

Well, that was bad news. On the bright side, Jovian was an orthodox Catholic Christian. One of the first things he did when he came back and started trying to get the empire back to normal was to invite Athanasius to return to Alexandria. In fact, all the exiles who had been banished by Constantius were called back, even the ones who had not come back in Julian's general amnesty.

Athanasius met Jovian at Antioch, and the new emperor was flatteringly hospitable. He immediately began to re-Christianize the empire, stopping the flow of public money to the pagan sacrifices, shutting the temples again, and supporting the Catholic Church so obviously that the Nicene Creed was suddenly very popular.

And then he died. He had reigned seven months.

The army chose an able commander named Valentinian to succeed him, and a month later, Valentinian made his brother Valens his co-emperor.

This was not good news.

Valens, a Rerun of Constantius

Valentinian, who took the western half of the empire as his domain, was a good Catholic, but Valens leaned toward the Arians. Valentinian was tolerant and didn't bother the Arians much. Valens was not tolerant.

Valens started his reign by persecuting the Nicene Christians in Antioch. He was distracted briefly by a usurper named Procopius, but after Procopius was defeated, Valens went back to his persecutions. He was looking more and more like Constantius, in fact, and in 365, he took the next logical step. He re-exiled all the bishops who had been banished by Constantius and reinstated by Julian. Sozomen tells us how Alexandria reacted:

> On account of this order, those who were at the head of the government of Egypt were anxious to deprive Athanasius of his bishopric and ex-

pel him from the city; for no light punishment was inserted in the imperial letters; for unless the injunctions were fulfilled, all the magistrates equally, and the soldiers under them, and counselors were condemned to the payment of much money and also threatened with bodily maltreatment.

The majority of Christians of the city, however, assembled and begged the governor not to banish Athanasius without further consideration of the terms of the imperial letter, which merely specified all bishops who had been banished by Constantius and recalled by Julian; and it was clear that Athanasius was not of this number, inasmuch as he had been recalled by Constantius and had resumed his bishopric; but Julian, at the very time that all the other bishops had been recalled, persecuted him, and finally Jovian recalled him. The governor was by no means convinced by these arguments; nevertheless, he restrained himself and did not give way to the use of force. The people ran together from every quarter; there was much commotion and perturbation throughout the city; an insurrection was expected; he therefore advised the emperor of the facts and allowed the bishop to remain in the city.

Some days afterwards, when the popular excitement had seemingly abated, Athanasius secretly left the city at dusk, and concealed himself somewhere. The very same night, the governor of Egypt and the military chief took possession of the church in which Athanasius generally dwelt, and sought him in every part of the building, and even on the roof, but in vain; for they had calculated upon seizing the moment when the popular commotion had partially subsided, and when the whole city was wrapped in sleep, to execute the mandate of the emperor, and to transport Athanasius quietly from the city.

Not to have found Athanasius naturally excited universal astonishment. Some attributed his escape to a special revelation from above; others to the advice of some of his followers; both had the same result; but more than human prudence seems to have been requisite to foresee and to avoid such a plot. Some say, that as soon as the people gave indications of being disposed to sedition, he concealed himself

among the tombs of his ancestors, being appre-
hensive lest he should be regarded as the cause
of any disturbances that might ensue; and that
he afterwards retreated to some other place of
concealment.[2]

According to Socrates Scholasticus, Athanasius lived for
four months in the tombs,[3] which were probably not
terribly uncomfortable. Wherever he was, he was out of
Alexandria.

This would be Exile Number Five.

8.
The Twist Ending

And that breaks the record. With five exiles, Athanasius is the most-exiled bishop in history. That doesn't count the number of times he had to run for his life temporarily, which is at least as many.

But Valens was not quite as obsessive as Constantius had been. Someone managed to persuade him that keeping Athanasius out of Alexandria wasn't worth the trouble. The people were rioting. The city was ungovernable without him.

So Valens relented after only a few months and

allowed Athanasius to come back. The historian Sozomen thought Valens would have preferred to keep Athanasius away but simply wasn't able. He also suggested that the Arians were afraid of him by that point. The Roman world was ruled by two emperors, and Valentinian in the West was staunchly pro-Athanasius. That had to be taken into consideration:

> It is very doubtful, whether, in making this concession, Valens acted according to his own inclination. I rather imagine that, on reflecting on the esteem in which Athanasius was universally held, he feared to excite the displeasure of the Emperor Valentinian, who was well-known to be attached to the Nicene doctrines; or perhaps he was apprehensive of a commotion on the part of the many admirers of the bishop, lest some innovation might injure the public affairs.
>
> I also believe that the Arian presidents did not, on this occasion, plead very vehemently against Athanasius; for they considered that, if he were thrown out of the city, he would probably betray them to the emperors and then would have an occasion for conference with respect to them, and might possibly succeed in persuad-

ing Valens to adopt his own sentiments, and in arousing the anger of the like-minded Valentinian against themselves.

They were greatly troubled by the evidences of the virtue and courage of Athanasius, which had been afforded by the events which had transpired during the reign of Constantius. He had, in fact, so skillfully evaded the plots of his enemies, that they had been constrained to consent to his reinstallation in the government of the churches of Egypt; and yet he could scarcely be induced to return from Italy, although letters had been dispatched by Constantius to that effect.

I am convinced that it was solely from these reasons that Athanasius was not expelled from his church like the other bishops, who were subjected to as cruel a persecution as ever was inflicted by pagans.[1]

Those who would not change their doctrinal tenets were banished; their houses of prayer were taken from them and placed in the possession of those who held opposite sentiments. Egypt alone was, during the life of Athanasius, exempted from this persecution.

Athanasius Returns

In the year 366, Athanasius returned from his fifth exile. He was old by then — probably at least sixty-eight — and he arrived home to find his church in disarray from decades of clerical upheaval and doctrinal confusion.

Once Lucius was gone, Athanasius had to return to putting his church back together. His program for reconstruction was simple, and it was little different from before. He kept telling the story. He kept rehearsing the doctrine.

And here is the twist ending of his story: Athanasius lived the rest of his life in peace, and when he died peacefully, he was surrounded by clergy and friends who loved and respected him.

After five exiles and at least as many sudden flights, after accusations of murder and rape and fiendish evil magic, after the rampaging of mobs through the streets, after death threats from emperors, Athanasius ended his life at peace with the world.

That doesn't mean the troubles were over in the Church. Far from it. But it does mean a merciful Providence gave Athanasius a taste of peace and rest after he had spent his life trying to keep a lid on chaos.

The storm broke as soon as Athanasius died:

The Arians had received early news of his death, so Euzoïus, president of the Arians at Antioch, and Magnus, the chief treasurer, were sent by the emperor, and lost no time in seizing and imprisoning Peter, whom Athanasius had appointed to succeed him in the bishopric; and they immediately transferred the government of the church to Lucius.

Hence those in Egypt suffered more grievously than those in other places, and misfortunes piled upon misfortunes oppressed the members of the Catholic Church; for as soon as Lucius settled in Alexandria, he attempted to take possession of the churches. He met with opposition from the people, and the clergy and holy virgins were accused as originators of the sedition. Some made their escape as if the city had fallen into the hands of an enemy; others were seized and imprisoned. Some of the prisoners were afterwards dragged from the dungeons to be torn with hooks and thongs, while others were burned by means of flaming torches. It seemed wonderful how they could possibly survive the tortures to which they were subjected. Banishment or even death itself would have been preferable to such sufferings

Peter, the bishop, made his escape from prison; and embarking on board a ship, proceeded to Rome, the bishop of which church held the same sentiments as himself.

Thus the Arians, although not many in number, remained in possession of the churches. At the same time, an edict was issued by the emperor, enacting that as many of the followers of the Nicene doctrines should be ejected from Alexandria and the rest of Egypt, as might be directed by Lucius. Euzoïus, having thus accomplished all his designs, returned to Antioch.[2]

There would be only a few years more of Arian trouble in the East. In 378, five years after Athanasius died, the bigoted Arian Valens was killed in battle against the Goths, and the orthodox Theodosius — remembered as Theodosius the Great — would take the throne and end the Arian domination of government. Athanasius would be remembered as the symbol of Catholic orthodoxy — the bishop who had held out against all odds, rallied the beleaguered forces of Christian truth, and given the Catholic Church the courage to survive.

The Summation

Athanasius's cause had seemed most unlikely to succeed. Arian Christology had government support. It was increasingly accepted by the bishops of the world. And bad things happened to those who opposed it.

Athanasius didn't care. He was resolute and unflinching. And he was prolific in his writing. He never tired of telling the story of the Arian controversy. He told it in numerous apologies and histories and letters, addressed to many audiences. To anyone who would listen, he would repeat the scriptural and theological arguments for the Nicene faith. His works are many, but (with only a few exceptions) they deal with the same problem, and they echo the same message of the coeternal Trinity and the coequality of the Divine Persons.

Athanasius adapted that message as Arianism produced other heresies. He lived to see some of his allies err by denying the divinity of the Holy Spirit. Thus, he had to marshal all his old arguments to demonstrate that neither the Son nor the Holy Spirit could do the things they do in Sacred Scripture if they had been anything less than fully divine.

In his long lifetime, Athanasius himself became symbolic — iconic, as we say today. His face was the face of the Council of Nicaea, with its creed and its introduction of the term *consubstantial* into the life of the Church. Thus, as the fortunes of Nicaea waxed and waned, Athanasius rose and fell. When emperors wanted to make peace with the Nicene party, they bestowed favors on Athanasius. But when emperors wanted to make trouble for the Nicene party, they made trouble for Athanasius. Unfortunately for our hero, the years of trouble were more numerous than the years of favor.

Athanasius lived to see a new generation of great theologians arise to explain and defend and even systematize the doctrine of Nicaea. They recognized Athanasius as the bastion of true doctrine when the storm of Arianism was raging.

The verdict of the Church at large has been the same. Catholic, Orthodox, and Protestant Christians have their disagreements, but this is one of the few things in Christian history they all agree on: Athanasius was right.

Could he have been more diplomatic? Perhaps. But perhaps there's not much time for diplomacy when your opponents are running around with a severed hand in a box, claiming you murdered one of their bishops. Perhaps there's not much time for diplomacy when hundreds of soldiers are beating down the door and shouting, "Where is Athanasius?" Athanasius's life was a life of emergencies. For most of it, he lived with an awareness that he might die at any moment. If he did die, he was going to die on the right side of the truth.

In that he succeeded. Today, when theologians want to speak of the *correct* doctrine of the Godhead, they specify the *Athanasian* doctrine.

And Athanasius could not possibly have wanted to be remembered any better way.

Acknowledgments

Thanks, as ever, to Christopher Bailey for the research assistance and new translations (from ancient Greek originals and modern French scholarship) — and for thirty-some years of friendship and collegiality.

Thanks to Roger Pearse (Tertullian.org) and Kevin Knight (NewAdvent.org), who gave me permission to quote freely from their archived ancient sources. I have used these public-domain sources, occasionally updating their language.

Thanks be to Mary Beth Giltner and the folks at OSV, who give me such enjoyable work.

Thanks be to God, who made such wonderful people as these and drew us all to a deep love of the Fathers.

Notes

1. The Boy Who Played Bishop

1. Sozomen, *Ecclesiastical History*, trans. Chester D. Hartranft, in *Nicene and Post-Nicene Fathers*, Second Series, vol. 2, ed. Philip Schaff and Henry Wace (Buffalo, NY: Christian Literature, 1890), 2.17.

2. Gregory Nazianzen, Oration 21, trans. Charles Gordon Browne and James Edward Swallow, in *Nicene and Post-Nicene Fathers*, Second Series, vol. 7, ed. Philip Schaff and Henry Wace (Buffalo, NY: Christian Literature, 1894).

3. Athanasius, *Life of St. Antony*, trans. Walter J. Burghardt (Westminster, MD: Newman Press, 1950), no. 21 (no. 44 in modern editions).

4. Julian, Letter 47, "To the Alexandrians," in *The Works of*

the Emperor Julian, vol. 3, trans. Wilmer Cave Francis Wright (London: Heinemann; New York: Macmillan, 1913).

2. Alexander's Right-Hand Man

1. Ammianus Marcellinus, *The Roman History of Ammianus Marcellinus, during the Reigns of the Emperors Constantius, Julian, Jovianus, Valentinian, and Valens*, trans. C. D. Yonge (London: G. Bell and Sons, 1902), 22.16.18.

2. Ammianus Marcellinus, *Roman History* 22.11.4.

3. Athanasius, *Contra Gentes* 1.16.

4. Athanasius quotes the lines in *Discourse 1 against the Arians* 2.5.

5. *Discourse 1 against the Arians* 2.7.

6. Athanasius, Epistle concerning the Councils (*De Synodis*), in *Select Treatises of S. Athanasius, Archbishop of Alexandria, in Controversy with the Arians*, trans. John Henry Newman (Oxford, UK: James Parker, 1877), 2.3.

7. Eusebius, *Life of Constantine* 2.68–70, in *Greek Ecclesiastical Historians of the First Six Centuries of the Christian Era* (London: Samuel Bagster, 1843), 2.68–70.

8. Ibid., *Life of Constantine* 2.73.

9. Ibid., *Life of Constantine* 3.8.

10. Ibid., *Life of Constantine* 3.12.

11. Ibid,, *Life of Constantine* 3.13.

12. Sozomen, *Ecclesiastical History* 1.17.

13. Ibid., *Ecclesiastical History* 1.20.

14. Ibid., *Ecclesiastical History* 1.21.

3. The Young Bishop

1. Theodoret, *A History of the Church in Five Books*, anonymous translation (London: Samuel Bagster and Sons, 1843), 1.27.

2. Note the wording that we recognize from the Creed we use today, suggesting that this was included and assumed in the original Nicene Creed.

3. Socrates Scholasticus, *Ecclesiastical History*, trans. A. C. Zenos, in *Nicene and Post-Nicene Fathers*, vol. 2, 1.26.

4. Athanasius, Epistle 1 to Serapion, in *The Letters of Saint Athanasius concerning the Holy Spirit*, trans. C. R. B. Shapland (London: Epworth Press, 1951).

5. Theodoret, *History of the Church* 1.26

6. Ibid., *History of the Church* 1.28.

7. Ibid., *History of the Church* 1.27.

8. Ibid., *History of the Church* 1.30.

9. This courtroom drama is pieced together from Socrates Scholasticus, *Ecclesiastical History* 1.29; Sozomen, *Ecclesiastical History* 2.25; and Theodoret, *History of the Church* 1.30.

10. Henry Hart Milman, *The History of Christianity: From the Birth of Christ to the Abolition of Paganism in the Roman Empire* (New York: T. Y. Crowell, 1881), 3.4.

11. Athanasius reproduces this letter in his *Apologia contra Arianos*, trans. M. Atkinson and Archibald Robertson, in *Nicene and Post-Nicene Fathers*, Second Series, vol. 4, eds. Philip Schaff and Henry Wace (Buffalo, NY: Christian Literature, 1892), 1.9.

4. Constantius Takes Over

1. Athanasius, *Letter 54 to Serapion*, trans. Archibald Robertson, in *Nicene and Post-Nicene Fathers*, vol. 4, 2–4.

2. Sozomen, *Ecclesiastical History* 3.2.

3. Ammianus Marcellinus, *Roman History* 21.16.18, new translation.

4. Sozomen, *Ecclesiastical History* 3.2.

5. Ibid., *Ecclesiastical History* 3.5.

6. Ibid., *Ecclesiastical History* 3.5.

7. Ibid., *Ecclesiastical History* 3.6.

8. Athanasius, *Encyclical Letter*, trans. M. Atkinson and Archibald Robertson, in *Nicene and Post-Nicene Fathers*, vol. 4, 2.

9. Athanasius, *Encyclical Letter* 3–5.

5. Support from the West

1. Sozomen, *Ecclesiastical History* 3.7.

2. Athanasius reproduces the letter in his *Apologia contra Arianos* 21–35.

3. Sozomen, *Ecclesiastical History* 3.7.

4. Jerome, Letter 127, 5, new translation.

5. Socrates Scholasticus, *Ecclesiastical History* 2.23.

6. Athanasius, *Apologia ad Constantium*, trans. M. Atkinson and Archibald Robertson, in *Nicene and Post-Nicene Fathers*, vol. 4, 4.

7. Ibid., *Apologia ad Constantium* 3.

8. Socrates Scholasticus, *Ecclesiastical History* 2.23.

9. Athanasius, *Apologia ad Constantium* 6.

10. Sozomen, *Ecclesiastical History* 4.9.

11. Ammianus Marcellinus, *Roman History* 15.8.6–10.

12. Sozomen, *Ecclesiastical History* 4.9.

13. Athanasius, *Apologia ad Constanium* 25.

6. Interesting Times

1. Sozomen, *Ecclesiastical History* 4.10.

2. Ibid., *Ecclesiastical History* 6.22.

3. Ammianus Marcellinus, *Roman History* 22.11.10.

4. Ibid., *Roman History* 22.5.3–4.

5. Julian, Letter 34, "To the Alexandrians, an Edict," in *The Works of Emperor Julian*, altered.

6. Julian, Letter 46, "To Ecdicius, Prefect of Egypt," in *The Works of Emperor Julian*, altered.

7. Julian, Letter 47, "To the Alexandrians," in *The Works of Emperor Julian*, altered.

7. A Brief Triumph

1. Socrates Scholasticus, *Ecclesiastical History* 3.14.

2. Sozomen, *Ecclesiastical History* 6.12.

3. Socrates Scholasticus, *Ecclesiastical History* 4.13.

8. The Twist Ending

1. Sozomen, *Ecclesiastical History* 6.12.

2. Ibid., *Ecclesiastical History* 6.19.

Bibliography

Ammianus Marcellinus. *The Roman History of Ammianus Marcellinus, during the Reigns of the Emperors Constantius, Julian, Jovianus, Valentinian, and Valens.* Translated by C. D. Yonge. London: G. Bell and Sons, 1902.

Ammianus Marcellinus and John Carew Rolfe. *Ammianus Marcellinus: With an English Translation by John C. Rolfe.* Rerum Gestarum Libri. English and Latin. Cambridge, MA: Harvard University Press; London: William Heinemann, 1935.

Athanasius. Epistle concerning the Councils (*De Synodis*). In *Select Treatises of S. Athanasius, Archbishop of Alexan-*

dria, in Controversy with the Arians. Translated by John Henry Newman. Oxford, UK: James Parker, 1877.

———. *The Letters of Saint Athanasius concerning the Holy Spirit*. Translated by C. R. B. Shapland. London: Epworth Press, 1951.

———. *The Life of Saint Antony*. Translated by Walter J. Burghardt. Westminster, MD: Newman Press, 1950.

———. *The Life of St. Antony*. Translated by Edward Stephens. London: Printed for the author, for the use and benefit of a religious Society, 1697.

———. *Select Treatises of St. Athanasius in Controversy with the Arians*. Translated by John Henry Newman. London: Longmans, Green, 1911.

Ayres, Lewis. "Not Two Things: Introducing the Incarnation in Eight Steps." *Church Life Journal*, December 14, 2021. https://churchlifejournal.nd.edu/articles /not-two-things-introducing-the-incarnation-in -eight-steps/.

Cavallera, Ferdinand. *Saint Athanase (295–373)*. Paris: Bloud, 1908.

Clifford, Cornelius. "Athanasius." *The Catholic Encyclopedia.* New York: Encyclopedia Press, 1913.

Greek Ecclesiastical Historians of the First Six Centuries of the Christian Era. London: Samuel Bagster, 1843.

A Harmony of Socrates, Sozomen, and Theodoret. Trans-

lated by A. C. Zenos, C. Hartranft, and B. Jackson. Fourth-Century Christianity. https://www
.fourthcentury.com/harmony-of-socrates-sozomen
-and-theodoret/.

Julian, Emperor of Rome. *The Works of the Emperor Julian.* Translated by Wilmer Cave France Wright. London: Heinemann; New York: Macmillan, 1913.

Milman, Henry Hart. *The History of Christianity: From the Birth of Christ to the Abolition of Paganism in the Roman Empire.* New York: T. Y. Crowell, 1881.

Quasten, Johannes. *Patrology: The Golden Age of Greek Patristic Literature.* Utrecht-Antwerp: Spectrum Publishers, 1960.

Roberts, Alexander, and James Donaldson. *Ante-Nicene Christian Library: Translations of the Writings of the Fathers down to A. D. 325.* Edinburgh: T. and T. Clark, 1867.

Schaff, Philip, and Henry Wace, eds. *A Select Library of Nicene and Post-Nicene Fathers of the Christian Church.* 14 vols. Buffalo, NY: Christian Literature, 1886–1890.

Theodoret. *A History of the Church in Five Books.* Anonymous translation. London: Samuel Bagster and Sons, 1843.

Weinandy, Thomas G., OFM Cap. *Athanasius: A Theological Introduction.* Washington, DC: Catholic University of America Press, 2018.

About the Author

Mike Aquilina is executive vice president and trustee of St. Paul Center for Biblical Theology. He is the award-winning author of more than fifty books on Catholic history, doctrine, and devotion. His works have been translated into many languages. His ongoing research is concerned with early Christian community and worship. He is past associate editor of *Scripture Matters*, the bulletin of the Institute of Applied Biblical Studies, and past editor of *New Covenant*, a Catholic spirituality magazine, and the *Pittsburgh Catholic*, the official newspaper of the Diocese of Pittsburgh. His reviews, essays, and journalism have appeared in *First Things*, *Touchstone*, *Crisis*, *National Catholic Register*, *Child and Family*, and elsewhere. Aquilina has hosted eleven television series and several documentary films and is a frequent guest on Catholic radio. He and his wife, Terri, live in the Pittsburgh area with their six children.

You might also like:

Fathers of the Faith: Saint Irenaeus
By Mike Aquilina

In this volume from OSV's *Fathers of the Faith* series, Mike Aquilina gives an overview of Irenaeus's life as a second-century Greek and the historical surroundings that affected his life and thought. A friend of Saint Polycarp from the same town in Asia Minor, Irenaeus was born in a Christian family and eventually became a bishop. His foundational works include *Against Heresies* and *The Demonstration of the Apostolic Preaching*, and these works remain relevant today.

More than 1,800 years after Irenaeus's death, Pope Francis has announced that he will be declared a Doctor of the Church, calling him "a great spiritual and theological bridge between Eastern and Western Christians."

Available at
OSVCatholicBookstore.com
or wherever books are sold

You might also like:

Fathers of the Faith: Saint Augustine
By Mike Aquilina

In this volume from OSV's *Fathers of the Faith* series, you'll be introduced to Saint Augustine of Hippo, including an overview of his life as a proud North African in the fourth and fifth century. His conversion from sinful young man to Catholic priest and bishop is well known from his autobiography, *Confessions*.

One of the four original Western Doctors of the Church, Augustine is considered the authority on almost everything because he wrote about practically everything. He incorporated the best of secular philosophy and science into his thought. His works are an encyclopedia of the Christian faith, and his writings have impacted countless millions. His legacy endures today.

You might also like:

Fathers of the Faith:
Saint John Chrysostom

By Mike Aquilina

In this accessible, bite-sized introduction, renowned author, speaker, and host Mike Aquilina gives an overview of John's life in Antioch and then Constantinople in the fourth and fifth centuries. Known to history as "golden-mouthed" because of his eloquent preaching, he is one of the most celebrated preachers of sermons in the history of the world and was also a prolific author. A Doctor of the Church, Saint John Chrysostom is remembered for his ascetical life and his courage. In the East, he is honored among the Three Holy Hierarchs. In the West, he is known as the Eucharistic Doctor. As archbishop of Constantinople, he was a figure of controversy, always in the middle of an argument with the powerful. He was a great figure in his time, and an even greater one after.

Available at

OSVCatholicBookstore.com

or wherever books are sold